Embracing The Sign

A Journey of Faith, Science, and Experience

T0191436

Embracing The Sign

A Journey of Faith, Science, and Experience

Marion Goldstein

P*

POLARIS PUBLICATIONS
St. Cloud, Minnesota

Cover art © iStock by Getty Images

Copyright © 2017 Marion Goldstein

ISBN: 978-1-68201-084-6 (paperback)
ISBN: 978-1-68201-088-4 (ebook)

Printed in the United States of America.

Published by:
Polaris Publications, an imprint of
North Star Press of St. Cloud, Inc.
Saint Cloud, Minnesota

www.northstarpress.com

Dedication

To my family—
for loving me enough
to allow me to tell these intimate stories
and to the others—
both friends and acquaintances
for trusting me
with theirs.

Acknowledgements

I would like to thank Sister Elizabeth Michael Boyle, O.P., for her shared insights and countless readings of the manuscript as it took shape. Thank you to Msgr. John Philip O'Connor, Mary Ladany, Joan Reamer, Kathleen Buse, and Linda Morgan for their probing questions and suggestions as first readers of the manuscript. And thank you to Dorothy Winheim, Wendy Dobler, and my children, Dennis Goldstein and Kathleen Zanowic, and my husband, Bob Goldstein, for their ongoing support and assistance.

Table of Contents

Part V
Consciousness

Part VI
Synthesis

Part VII
Synchronicity

Part VIII
Consciousness: The Link between Science & Religion

Part IX
Signs

Part X
Tying It All Together: The Interface of Faith, Science, and Personal Experience

Introduction

THIS MEMOIR includes a collection of personal stories about ordinary people who had extraordinary experiences following the death of a loved one. Each recounts a confluence of events or a series of coincidences that could not have been planned for or anticipated, but seem to come from "out of the blue." What makes these stories important is the profound effect the experience had on those involved. Each person found reassurance in the occurrence and an overwhelming sense that death was not the end, that the deceased continued to exist in some form, apart from and beyond the death of the body.

The power of each story is conveyed through the idiosyncratic, personal and inexplicable way everyday objects—a letter, a belt, a balloon, a meat thermometer, a song, a book, a light fixture, the sash to a dress—become a vehicle through which a reassuring message is communicated. In each case, the object is interpreted as a sign, since it represents a shared history between the living and the dead, a history known only to them. Sometimes humorous, sometimes serious, these signs are experienced as something spiritual. They point to an unimaginable "more" capable of breaking through the boundaries separating life and death, and making itself known to the living.

A common thread running through these stories is the sense of presence conveyed by the experience, a sense that the deceased is present in that moment and a sense that a spiritual world exists.

This is comingled with feelings of peace and comfort, however short lived, that mediate grief and the pain of separation so prevalent immediately after a death. A second thread embedded in each story is the power of love, suggesting that love is a force that binds us in a universe that scientists increasingly find more complex and eternal than they ever imagined.

As I both lived through such experiences and accumulated stories from others, awe and wonder wrestled with the skeptic in me. I continued to ask: What is happening here? For some, these events were merely random acts of coincidence that would eventually be explained through science and natural law. For others, they were evidence of magical thinking or projections of the mind created to fulfill a psychological need. For those who had had such experiences, they were seen as wordless and powerful communications from a spiritual world that reflected an afterlife.

Friends and acquaintances often asked what I was writing about. After I told them it was about signs after death, the response was often, "Do I have a story for you. I never told anyone before, but maybe it'll help you with your book." Many of the experiences people related had happened years before, but they remained integrated as peak moments that still informed the storytellers' relationship with death.

As I discovered how common these coincidental experiences were, I began to research possible explanations. Beginning with the paranormal, one field of inquiry led to another and took me into cosmology, psychology, quantum physics, and theology. Since all experiences, perceptions, beliefs, feelings, and actions are filtered through our consciousness, I was drawn first to psychology, psychiatry, and neuroscience. And because many of these experiences were integrated in a spiritual context, I also was drawn to theology.

Scientists and theologians ask many of the same questions about ultimate meanings, beginnings and endings, creation and death. Both disciplines are concerned with how life begins, how a single cell becomes a thinking human being, and what happens to human consciousness when we die.

Science demands rigorous proof. Theology and the realm of the supernatural make no such demands. Yet storylines seemed not only to converge but also to embrace one another. Nowhere is this more evident than in the scientific and theological questions posed by death and the afterlife.

These questions led me to scientists and theologians delving into such questions within their own disciplines. I found the work fascinating, inspiring, affirming. I have attempted to comingle my personal interest and experience with stories of signs and the writings of a new breed of theologians finding science compatible with spirituality. They have integrated modern science into their theology, and, in so doing, embark on a new avenue to spirituality.

Since I am neither a scientist nor a theologian, I have relied on the words of respected scientists and theologians. I limited myself to those whose words spoke to me in my efforts to advance my own faith in an afterlife, which, for me, was the main criteria of a belief in God. I have integrated their words with my own and included a bibliography to reference direct quotes that are a product of their expertise.

At the same time, I acknowledge that I have not included the mainstream scientific belief successful in removing God from the picture. For me God still exists.

This is a book for those whose spiritual interests allow them to consider science as a valid form of inquiry into the existence of God. It is for those who find themselves rejecting or doubting God because science has "disproved" or "undermined" much of the dogma and doctrine that, up until the latter half of the twentieth century, formed the underpinnings of their belief in God. It is for those who question and wonder about life after death.

In the end, this book weaves together my own spiritual journey from blind faith to skeptic to the ultimate discovery that a fragile faith can be found, and found again, in the questions.

Disclaimer

Although this book contains references, direct and indirect, to the theologians and scientists who have been my companions on my faith journey, I assume that the reader, like me, is not an academic. All that I claim as my own are the ways I have used these authors in reaction to my experiences and the true stories I have gathered. Therefore, to avoid both plagiarism and burdening the text with full bibliographical documentation, I have chosen simply to identify the author and include a bibliography and make the rest available at my website to anyone who requests it.

Part I

The Beginning

Chapter 1

Good-bye

THE TEACHER ANNOUNCED our second-grade class was going to visit a classmate, Christine, to say good-bye. "Christine won't be taking her seat anymore. Christine has died," she said to the hushed rows of children, seated properly in alphabetical order. I looked over to the empty seat at the third desk in the first row. Christine, with her red curls and freckles, had been sitting there only a few days ago. "Everyone move up a seat," Sister Mary Immaculata said as she instructed the children in the first row to fill in at the empty desk. Wordlessly, they moved, a slight shift in the geography of the classroom. "Christine is in heaven," Sister Immaculata assured us. "She is with God and the angels where she will be perfectly happy forever. We will be going to say good-bye to her after lunch."

That afternoon the class of sixty students, now fifty-nine, was led across the street to Christine's house. As we approached the front door, we heard crying that filtered down from the house and grew louder with each approaching step.

I lived several blocks away in that Brooklyn neighborhood of criss-crossing streets and brick stoops where distance predicted friendships. I had never been to Christine's house before. Christine was in the living room. All the furniture was gone. Enormous sprays of floral arrangements covered the walls from floor to ceiling. We had been instructed to file slowly past the open casket with our eyes downcast and say a prayer to our classmate who was now with God. I peeked. Christine looked exactly as she had the day she made her First Holy Communion, except she was lying down. She didn't look sick, as I had expected. Her white dress and veil were spread across a white satin pillow. Pearl rosary beads were laced around her fingers. I swear I saw her small chest rise and fall beneath the white dress. *This is all a mistake,* I thought. But no one else seemed to notice, and Christine remained dead.

The flowers, looming in the living room, were grotesque in their enormity. The overwhelming odor of those floral sprays mingled with the crying coming from the other room. The scent attached itself like a barnacle to some synapse in my brain, because I have never again looked at cut flowers without a whiff of death filling my nostrils. But as for Christine, I followed my teacher's instructions. Assured that she was perfectly happy with God, I did not think of her.

Yet, I thought of myself. I did not want to die. A small fear grew inside me. I did not want to catch a burst appendix! I did not want to leave my mother, even if I was to be perfectly happy with God. I did not want my mother to cry the way Christine's mother was crying in the kitchen. And I could not help but wonder what Christine was going to do in heaven for all eternity.

For a child, so much of happiness depends on having a desire met—for a trip to the circus, a bicycle, a best friend to play with, a new dress, no school because it's snowing. Simple things. For other seven-year-olds the desire may be more complicated—for bullying to end, a parent to stop drinking, shame to disappear. Yet in both scenarios, happiness seems to depend on time. Without time to fulfill desire, existence seems static, the flat line of a horizon that never changes. Everlasting sameness. And at seven years old, I had all the time in the world. At least eternity would be shorter for me than it was for Christine, I thought, as I dismissed it as something for other people.

Even before Christine died, the concept of God and heaven had been reinforced each day, along with the times tables, pronouns, and the Pledge of Allegiance. It was a truth written on the blackboard below the laminated alphabet, displayed in both cursive and print, rimming the high-ceilinged classroom. Washed clean of the previous day's chalk dust, the catechism question shone white on the blackboard.

Q. Why are you here? (*Here*, it was understood, was not simply being in the classroom on that particular day. *Here* was "to exist.")

A. To know, love and serve God on this earth and be happy with him in heaven.

There it was, the recipe for life. Contained in the little sentence excerpted from the *Baltimore Catechism*, the fact of God, the fact of heaven. No questions asked. Heaven was in the cards. All one had to do was toe the line and love God. Not a very difficult admonition. No more difficult than memorizing the exports of the United States and the difference between a verb and an adverb. This was the undertow of my Catholic education.

SIX YEARS LATER, infinity shook me. My friends and I were discussing a math class. A girlfriend traced the mathematical symbol for infinity on paper napkins and illustrated how there was no escape from it. The old oak table in the Brooklyn ice cream parlor, the chocolate egg cream, and the straw standing upright in the glass are all anchors to my thirteen-year-old self that day. Frightening thoughts about death and infinity, a concept that, until that moment, had been relegated to the study of math, sprang from some dormant seed within me.

For a Catholic girl attending an all girls' Catholic high school, the promise of an afterlife, in a place called heaven, was unquestionable in the faith in which I had been reared. The moment of that off-hand remark in the Brooklyn ice cream parlor drew me into a labyrinth. For the first time, I literally confronted eternity. Time without end, to go on and on and on was ungraspable, unimaginable, and frightening. The thought caused my head to swim and a vague nausea to make its way through my body as a subtle panic set in. The smell of flowers, a white First Holy Communion dress, and Christine erupted in my memory.

I did what I imagine most thirteen-year-old girls do. I pushed the thought aside and got back to the chocolate egg cream, the boy in the next booth, and the teenage realities so important at the time. No one else I knew had died, although the whisperings of other kids, polio, iron lungs, and the boy around the corner, who couldn't walk, loomed in the shadow of my awareness. It had been seven years since Christine died, and I had continued to live. I was probably going to live forever!

Time went on, infused with a revolving set of desires, all of which could be accomplished while loving God. As an adolescent, it was a perfect math score, an invitation to dance, a diploma, a room of my own, unblemished skin, a trip to Radio City Music Hall. This was the time of preparation, the anteroom of life. Serving God would come later.

As a young woman growing up in the sixties, I had two choices: become a nun or follow in my mother's footsteps and marry. In marriage I could serve God by rearing Catholic babies, who in turn "would know, love and serve God and be happy with him in heaven."

I chose marriage when I was barely twenty-one years old. I had known Bob, a neighborhood boy, since eighth grade. When pregnancy didn't happen in the first six months of our marriage, I made an appointment with a doctor. Surely there was something wrong with me. I prayed the rosary each day to Mary, the mother of God, to fulfill my burning desire to be a mother. Driving home from a movie or a party on a Saturday night, Bob and I recited the prayers together, one of the most intimate acts of our marriage. We were in it together, counting on God to help us create the blueprints of the life we would build together.

And it happened. Whether prayers were answered or nature took its course, within the next five years I gave birth to my three oldest children. Each filled me with a joy beyond what I could ever have imagined. By the time I was in my mid-twenties, the objects of my desire, my way of serving God, what He wanted for me, aligned perfectly with what I wanted.

Yet, I was increasingly preoccupied with the fear of losing my children, whether literally at the playground or the Thanksgiving

Day parade, in a car crash if I weren't present in my imagined omnipotence to protect them, or to a fever that spiraled out of control. My anxiety about their safety burned obsessively. Life was fragile, and I saw danger at every turn. My vague feelings about my own death and eternity crystallized, the way minerals dispersed throughout the substrata of bedrock become the hard black rocks of coal. In my vigilance to avoid death, I thought about it all the time.

It was exhausting. I kept track of children who were diagnosed with leukemia, children who fell out of windows, and children who drowned when a parent looked away. A good friend once commented that I had nightmares all day long. Gradually my fears overshadowed all the little things that had brought me happiness. I would not let my children out of my sight. Even a trip to the grocery store with their father caused me to watch the clock and monitor the minutes until their return. Even when my own children were safely tucked in their beds at night, I was becoming exquisitely aware of a world in which safety and happiness were reserved for the lucky few. My provincial views garnered from the safety of a happy childhood had gradually telescoped to include a world where poverty, inequality, war, and evil were endured, day in and day out by the many, with no hope of any amelioration. In my unrelenting preoccupation, literally everything in life led to death; everything in life was meaningless.

As I struggled to find my way in my search for meaning, my reason for being, an incredible sadness overcame me. My world grew smaller and smaller. As I fought the overwhelming panic, the God whom all my life I had accepted on blind faith vanished. I was truly lost. The existential questions that had eluded me while I was busy changing diapers and running after toddlers pounded like surf in my brain.

What is it all about?

Is there a God?

Is there an afterlife?

If there is no afterlife, does anything matter?

Is life an absurd joke?

PRAYER HAD ALWAYS been my answer, the current that moved me forward. I had prayed to pass exams, for the phone to ring, the bus to come, my brother to return from Vietnam. I had prayed to St. Jude for the impossible, St. Gerard to become pregnant, St. Anthony for loss, St. Patrick for luck. And my prayers had been answered. I had everything I wanted, or so it seemed. But now prayer was empty. The whole idea of life being about an afterlife, of a heaven or hell for eternity, was cast into doubt. I could not find God.

I could not pray my way out of this one. As my anxiety and hopelessness increased, physical symptoms manifested themselves. I awoke each day at four in the morning and tried to intellectualize my way out of the joylessness that had overtaken me. I lost the ability to eat; weight fell from my body. I craved sleep, the only release from my swirling obsessive thoughts. After getting the three children to bed, I would crash, only to awaken at 4:00 a.m. with hours of empty minutes, heavy with obsessive thoughts, ahead of me. I tried to make my life meaningful, fill the hours with a job selling Avon, volunteering with the Red Cross and the Probation Department, but the existential questions kept pounding away at me. *What is it all about, this life that ends in death?*

I didn't know what was wrong with me. I feared I was going crazy. I had everything I thought I wanted: a home, a husband, and three children I loved more than life itself. Yet every hour of every day was an ordeal to be gotten through. Time crawled. Minutes dragged as my brain tried to work its way out of my inability to find happiness or joy in anything. The pain of depression was unlike anything I had ever experienced. I would have willingly traded it for physical pain, which I knew I could bear. I prayed to the God who wasn't there. *Just let me survive until my youngest child is eighteen and doesn't need me anymore.*

This may have been the craziest thought I had, but at the time it kept me functioning through the unrelenting void of depression. But to have missed the rest of my life, the days and years that lay ahead of me, is a thought that even today, all these years later, causes me to shiver.

But the picture that would become my one and only precious life was hidden from me then, concealed the way swirls of oil paint on an artist's pallette hide the uncountable brush strokes that will go into creating an original canvas. All the small things that enhance life, as well as the large, were beyond my imagination. Like the simple savoring of a perfect corned-beef sandwich, the amazing flow of a game of tennis when body and mind are coordinated perfectly, the awe of peering into the dizzying depths of a crevasse on a glacier in Alaska, the unparalleled joy of sharing life with my children as they grew into adulthood and became my best friends, it was all potential waiting to be embodied.

Once, when I was still young enough, I fantasized myself as Katherine Hepburn rowing through a tangled jungle in the movie *African Queen*. It was early April when I commandeered an old canoe and paddled into a swamp that hid between the shallow rims of Lake Wanda and Lake Wawayanda. I left the canoe moored in a corridor of cattails and entered a cove of trees, wading knee deep in murky water. The slender winter branches of a willow provided a scaffold I climbed. From a high vantage I saw millions of brown buds, each closed tight as a fist. When suddenly the sun broke through the early morning fog and began to roll over the morning, I heard before I saw the cracking open of the winter willows' hard bud kernels. The sun shone as bud after bud sang itself into a shimmering dome as the wooly catkins burst, transforming the swamp with a silver iridescence.

That moment, which I came to call the epiphany of the swamp, holds me still. It serves as a living metaphor for the way a life can sing itself into itself, bud by bud, experience by experience. But what this experience would mean to me came much later.

At the time of my craziest thought, it was the late sixties. Treatment for mental illness had not yet entered the mainstream. There was a stigma, a shame attached to engaging in psychotherapy and psychiatry. Yet, the day came when frightening and unknown as it was, I knew I needed help. I could not help myself.

I started with a priest who was wise enough to recommend a psychiatrist. During my first visit, clinical depression was diagnosed. I was given a prescription for medicine and referred to a therapist. I was unable to tolerate the medicine, but the psychotherapist to whom I was referred would become my anchor to myself during the next five years.

One of the first insights gained in the early months of therapy was that motherhood was the solution I had created for a meaningful life. My identity was built around motherhood, just like my own mother's was and like Mary, the mother of God. Since I had not been able to become pregnant again, my life was losing its meaning. Without being able to sustain my chosen identity, who was I?

Suffusing all this was my preoccupation with the fragility of life, the constant vigilance to avoid death and the unattractiveness of an afterlife that spoke to my diminished faith.

The therapist suggested that my desire for a pregnancy be held in abeyance until I could get my fears and anxieties about death and the meaning of life under control. This did not seem like a difficult request. I had thought pregnancy was the answer long before I started therapy and it hadn't happened. There was no reason to think I was going to conceive now.

I was in therapy less than a year when I found myself pregnant. I was both scared and pleased. Scared because I knew how my unresolved anxieties still kept me emotionally fragile and pleased because a part of me still believed bringing children into the world was where meaning lay. With meaning, the questions eating away at me would dissolve, like soap bubbles down a drain.

The therapist didn't see it that way. I can still see the look of concern and disappointment on his face as he calculated the time it would take for us to get back to the questions I was grappling with now that a new baby was on the way.

It would be that pregnancy, my fourth and final one, that thrust me even deeper into the core questions breaking me apart.

Chapter 2

The Myth of Motherhood
1970

"We are not human beings having a spiritual experience, we are spiritual beings having a human experience."
Pierre Teilhard de Chardin

I CONTINUED WITH THERAPY. Each Monday morning when the two older children, Robert and Kathy, were in school, my trusted girlfriend and neighbor took care of Dennis. I drove myself to a town about twenty miles away to keep my appointment. It was a town where nobody knew me or my shame-filled diagnosis. My anxieties multiplied to include this new being I was carrying inside me. *Let this baby be healthy, let this baby be normal* was the mantra and prayer, the beat behind my thoughts.

And then one morning as I was pushing the vacuum cleaner, I had a feeling I had not experienced before. A huge fist was tightening in my abdomen. I turned the vacuum off and lay down on the couch. My abdomen relaxed. I mentioned it to the doctor on my next visit. He was unconcerned.

But a week later, as I sat in the kitchen with the children, who had come in for lunch, I suddenly felt wetness through my maternity dress. Thinking one of the children had spilled milk, I got up to examine the puddle on the oak chair. But no, it wasn't milk; the fluid was coming from me. My water had broken. It was June 12, 1970, six full weeks before my due date.

As Bob sped down the highway on the way to the emergency room, I lay with my legs raised across the back seat. I contracted my every pelvic muscle, trying to hold back the flow of water seeping from my womb. Alongside the roadway, spring trees were in various stages of greening. A clump of dogwood blossomed in a blaze of white light. Surely nothing could die on such a day. No sooner had the thought formed in my mind than another, dark and ominous, emerged. How during this pregnancy, as in the three earlier pregnancies, I refused to prepare in a concrete way for the baby. There had been no purchasing of diapers or tiny shirts or anything else in advance of the birth. There were no baby showers. Names had been considered and rejected, but each of my children remained nameless until after taking their first breath. Always there was the awareness of what could go wrong, the misguided notion that I could protect myself from shattering if I did not accumulate a stash of things I might not be able to use. I appeased the gods of misfortune by taking nothing for granted. It had worked. When the other children were born, it was Bob who did the last-minute shopping in the hours before I brought the baby home. Not preparing had produced good results. My thoughts careened back and forth between the yin and yang of my unborn baby's destiny.

In the emergency room, I was scared as a nurse handed me her stethoscope. "Here, listen to the heartbeat. It's strong for eight months, very strong."

Oh, joy. The rhythm of the heart amidst the swooshing fluid was like nothing I had ever heard before.

The doctor injected my arm with a solution. "Count backward from ten," he said.

By the time I got to seven I was slurring, and at five I slipped into a deep well of timelessness. I awoke several hours later in a stainless-steel recovery room. I felt my belly—the swell of child was gone, shrunken as a dried-out pumpkin.

An aide sat at the foot of the bed reading.

"How's my baby?" I asked.

"Go back to sleep. The doctor will be in later to talk to you."

"What did I have, a boy or girl?"

"You had a boy."

"Is he okay?"

"Go to sleep. The doctor will talk to you later."

"Please tell me. Is he okay?

Silence.

"Were you there? Did you see him? Did he cry? He was six weeks early."

Silence.

"Please tell me."

"I can't. It's the rule. You have to wait for the doctor."

She did not deviate from her script. I could hear the pages of the magazine ripple as this programmed robot in green scrubs methodically turned them. I thought I would go mad.

Again, I begged, "Is he alive?"

"You have to wait for the doctor. He's with him now."

"What time is it?"

"It is the middle of the night."

There are moments in life that are meaningful in idiosyncratic ways, moments infused with an insight unexplainable in its power to inform our deepest selves. You can't plan them the way you can plan a wedding or a picnic. Nor can you produce them with intent or will. Revelatory in deeply personal ways, these experiences can't be had secondhand. They are moments that strike directly at the heart of truth and lift you above yourself in a joyous ascent of the heart that can neither be sustained nor repeated.

Yet the memory lingers. Imprinting itself like a primitive etching on a cave wall, buried under the mountain of experience that both precedes and follows, it shines, it beckons. Often ineffable, these moments beg to be told, extracted from the myriad experiences of "life lived" and chiseled into words.

This was such a moment. Suddenly I knew. I didn't know what I knew, but here was the part that I will never forget. From the spotlight over the gurney, a knowledge as clear and hard as a diamond entered my whole being. A Presence filled the room. It flowed into me as pure knowledge.

"Your baby is no more. There is a reason. You do not know it, but it will unfold."

An astonishing peace filled me. It probably lasted no more that a minute before I was wild with fear again. Yet on some level it lasted forever, and in my darkest moments, I returned to that Presence when there was nowhere else to go. This part of my experience matched no other, a transcendence that could never be undone. I didn't know it then, but its power would serve as the bedrock for what was to come.

I lay awake, waiting. A pediatrician I had never seen before approached the bed. "I'm sorry," he said. "Your baby's lungs were not strong enough. We tried, but we couldn't save him. The doctor is calling your husband now." In retrospect, he was telling me what had already been revealed to me.

"How long was he alive?

"For about eleven hours."

The pediatrician made a move to leave my bedside. The aide had already left the room.

"Was he baptized?" I asked.

"Yes, your husband had him baptized right after you gave birth."

I wanted to prolong the conversation, keep the pediatrician there with me, talking about those eleven hours when my baby existed, before the door to the future had closed. He left.

A few minutes later, a nurse came into the room. "What do you want to name him?"

I could hardly believe the question. What was the point? I would never sing to him or call him in from the backyard or cheer for him on a basketball court.

I was silent. I did not want to name him. In those moments, in my ignorance, I wanted to deny, obliterate, forget his sudden eruption into this world of two brothers and a sister, of little flannel kimonos with silk ribbons that I planned to sew for him.

"We need a name for the death certificate," she said. And so I chose John, a name devoid of personal meaning to me. I falsely believed it would be the easiest to relinquish, the easiest to forget. My baby would be a John, a John Doe, an unknown child I must forget.

"Do you want to hold him?" the nurse asked me.

"No," I said, in what was probably the biggest mistake of my life. I was afraid to touch his tiny, cold, dead body that had been struggling to survive for the last eleven hours without me, afraid to look into that face that was so closed to me, a face I would spend the rest of my life imagining. I looked at the light above the gurney. I willed the Presence that had flooded me earlier to return, to no avail; it was over.

I YEARNED TO KNOW what happened to me in that hospital room. I asked myself if I had had a spiritual experience, whatever that was. Did it matter what I called it? The reality was it happened, and it caused an internal change in me. That was enough.

I told no one except my husband, fearing others might judge the experience, find trivial what was so intimate and important to me. I wanted to hold onto it, keep it from slipping away, like mercury, into myriad tiny pieces.

As time went on, the immediate power of those moments in the recovery room dissipated, but the change it wrought within me has survived and made a difference for the rest of my life. Those who have made a study of the mind write of peak experience, those rare and exquisite moments that stand in bold relief to all the rest, where a sense of oneness and a connectedness to all that is causes everything else to fall away. So it was for me.

My son John died on June 13, 1970. His brief life and death changed everything. The myth of motherhood I had chosen, or which had chosen me, was short-circuited. The worst thing I thought could happen had happened. I believed I could not survive such grief. But I was still alive. It had not killed me. I was still getting up each day to get the children off to school, to cook their meals, to soothe their hurts. Yet every action was suffused with the loss of what could have been, what was—for eleven ruptured hours.

Emotionally, I did not have the courage to carry another child inside me for nine months, to grow to love that child the way I grew to love my John, knowing that the same fate could befall another pregnancy. And hadn't my therapist told me that pregnancy was not the immediate solution for the anxieties that consumed me?

In September, the three children went off to school wearing their new shoes and carrying shiny new bookbags. I watched the crossing guard on the corner shepherd them across the street. Still in my nightgown, and without plan or forethought, I ignored the bowls of half-eaten cereal pieces floating in puddles of milk that lingered on the kitchen table, and the to-do list of errands and odd jobs I had planned to squeeze into the morning. I climbed the stairs and threw myself onto the bed, truly alone for the first time all summer. There was no one to protect from my tears, no child banging the screen door looking for a cookie. There would be no interruption until the children returned for lunch three hours later. I heard myself sobbing. Unbidden, accumulated tears came and came. I couldn't stop them. And for the first time, I didn't try to stop them. Only years later would I came to appreciate the healing power of tears, the storm that must take place before light can get through the clouds. But at that time I was just allowing myself to be myself. For over two hours I cried with abandon.

At some point I reached for an envelope on the nightstand and rummaged through a drawer for a pencil in the still, shade-darkened bedroom. I began writing to the baby I could not hold in my arms, a spontaneous rush of words erupted onto the paper.

Dearest John,
I wonder, oh my little one, if you know how much you're loved . . .

A poem poured forth from the deepest part of my being, a simple poem about a mother and the son she could not have. I had never written a poem before, nor had I ever even thought about doing so, but as if possessed, I found myself scribbling madly on the back of the envelope. I was writing toward something. I didn't know what it was until I put the pencil down and read what I had written.

Now, staring me in the face from the back of the envelope were all my ambiguities about God, about a place called heaven and my child who may or may not exist in another dimension. My own words revealed a flash of faith, deeply overshadowed with doubt, in the existence of another world, and the futility of trying to comprehend it in this one.

I was flooded with the existential questions about the meaning of life. My power to protect my children from harm had exploded in John's death. The worst had happened, and I had been impotent to stop it. Not prayer, not love, not intention had altered the course of events. I yearned to know this infant I had carried within me the previous seven months, whose little fist or foot I had felt in my palm as it rippled the flesh of my belly. With the realization I would never know him in this life, questions about an afterlife loomed as they never had before, reflecting my own inner conflict. I had my faith, or so I thought, which included heaven. Yet heaven seemed an abstraction, a realm relegated to images, albeit lovely images where God existed and my lost son with Him.

Could I believe that?

I yearned for more, an assurance my dead son's brief existence meant something and I would know him in another reality. Like doubting Thomas, who would not believe in the resurrected Lord until he put his hands to the wounds, I yearned for something to reconcile being and non-being. Now I desperately wanted to believe in an afterlife, not because I had memorized sentences about it from a catechism, but because I had come to it through my own experience, my own consciousness. I didn't know where to start.

Part II

Investigating

Chapter 3

Living the Questions
1970 to 1975

"Live the questions now. Perhaps you will then gradually, without noticing it, live along some distant day into the answer."

Rilke

E VEN IF I DID NOT KNOW WHERE to start, to some extent I
had already started. I had been confronting death in therapy sessions since before becoming pregnant with John.
For the last several months, that quest, which seemed to underlie
all my anxieties, was deferred as I prepared for this baby whose
responsibility it would be to infuse my life with new meaning.

Only in retrospect was I able to see the avalanche of riches
put into motion by John's death. Only in looking back was I able
to see the gifts this child, who came and went like a meteor in the
night, left in his wake.

"There is a reason. You do not know it. But it will unfold." The
words sustained me through every "Why? Why?" They were not
words but a personal experience of something more, something
providential, something intimating God. Like a prophecy fulfilled, in the years ahead I would adopt my two youngest sons,
discover poetry and learn to rely on its sustaining power, become
trained as a poetry therapist, go on to earn an advanced degree
in psychology and embark on a career as a psychotherapist, all of
which filled my life with meaning.

But that was much later. In the months after my baby's death, I was caught in a vortex spiraling downward. In addition to therapy, I turned to religion for answers.

I read *The Dark Night of the Soul*, a cornerstone of Catholic belief written by St. John of the Cross. The title drew me in. Comprehending the theology was another thing, akin to diving into the deep end of the pool without knowing how to swim. I flailed and grasped at the concepts. Yet there was a strange comfort just relating to the title. At least I knew I was not alone.

I wrote to Dr. Norman Vincent Peale, the guru of positive thinking. He wrote back, or rather his assistant responded with a neatly typed letter of encouragement and faith. In spite of the generous intention, it did little to move me forward in my quest to come to terms with death.

I joined an interfaith group, thinking exposure to another religion's way of comprehending God would open a door for me. The discussions centered on differences and similarities in the respective faiths. People spoke of how they experienced God in their lives.

I listened with envy, feeling like an imposter, my presence in the room a pretense, attesting to a faith that I *wanted* to possess but didn't. One evening, after the discussion ended and the hostess was pouring tea and coffee and offering the requisite cookies, she turned toward me and casually asked, "How do you experience God in your life?"

Tears collected behind my eyes. My voice faltered. I could not pretend to share the religious enthusiasm of the others. Their unquestioning reliance on scripture and dogma was beyond me. Could I confess my raging doubts, my endless questions, my sense of shame and desertion that left me on the outside of all that once embraced me?

"I wish I had your faith, but I just don't," I simply said.

Chatter in the room ceased. I can still see the forkful of chocolate cake, frozen mid-air, on its way to the mouth of a woman trying to find the words to pull me back into the fold. She didn't know what to say to me.

I didn't feel judged, just pitied, but I never went back to the group. What sustained me, what kept me going was the experience in the recovery room after John's death. It would not be until many years later that I would come across the words of the theologian Karl Rahner, who in his book *Christians Living Formerly and Today* validated my amorphous intuitions. "The devout Christian of the future will either be a mystic, *that is one who has experienced something,* or will cease to be anything at all." (Italics are mine) Rahner did not attempt to categorize that something, like the one hundred Eskimo words for snow. Rather, he left it open ended and personal. He left room for me.

With trepidation, lest I be judged unstable, or worse, diagnosed psychotic, I eventually told my therapist about my experience in the recovery room.

"Did you ever hear of anything like that before? Do you think I'm crazy?" I asked.

He didn't think I was crazy. He didn't know what happened to me in that recovery room, but clearly something had happened. "Something shifted inside of you, enlarged your consciousness," he said. "How else can you account for that brief moment when you were lifted out of despair to momentarily accept your worst fear?"

"Do you think it was a spiritual experience?" I tentatively asked him.

He didn't know but asked me, "Have you ever read *The Variety of Religious Experiences* by William James?"

I had a vague memory of hearing about William James, not so much for his accomplishments but because he was the older brother of the great American novelist Henry James, whom I read in high school literature classes. Now I learned that William James was a renowned figure in his own right. His academic career was spent at Harvard University, where he taught anatomy, philosophy, physiology, biology, and psychology. Known as the Father of American Psychology, he began his career at Harvard in 1876 and retired in 1907, three years before his death in 1910. During these years, psychology was first considering itself a science and James was drawn to the scientific study of the mind. *The Variety of Religious Experiences*, thought to be his most important work, was his study of consciousness.

The text of the *The Varieties of Religious Experience* was taken from the Gifford Lectures, a series of twenty lectures he delivered at the University of Edinburgh in Scotland in 1901 and 1902 and first published in London in 1902. Since then, they have been republished over and over again, and have never been out of print. Today, one hundred and fifteen years later, the Kindle edition has made *The Variety of Religious Experiences* available in the farthest corners of the globe.

I bought a paperback copy on my way home from the appointment. I quickly determined that in its density, it was not the kind of book I could read cover to cover. Actually, my grief and anxieties were so debilitating I did not have the attention span to read any book in its entirety. Rather, I immediately scanned the index for a chapter or subtitle that would take me directly to a topic that might speak to my experience in the recovery room.

Chapter 4

Presence
1971

*"The best part of every mind is not that which a person knows,
but that which hovers in gleams, suggestions tantalizing un-
possessed before him."*   Emerson

U NDER "CONSCIOUSNESS OF GOD" in a chapter James entitled "Mysticism," I found what I was looking for. Here
were first-person accounts of men and women from all
walks of life recounting their religious and spiritual experiences. Ordinary and extraordinary people, from the bobby walking the streets
of London, to the saints of Christianity, to the sacred texts of the
Hindu religion written in 1000 B.C.E.; all described religious and
spiritual experiences and all told of being changed as a result.

One of the first accounts I read confessed, "The highest experiences that I have had of God's presence have been rare and
brief . . . flashes of consciousness which have compelled me to ex-
claim with surprise . . . God is here." Another, which seemed pre-
scient of the science that the second half of the twentieth century
would examine, wrote, "I saw the universe is not composed of
dead matter, but is on the contrary a Living Presence; I became
conscious of myself in eternal life . . . I saw that all men are
immortal . . ."

All of these testaments spoke to a knowing, manifested in
each individual's consciousness by the sense of a Divine Presence

23

that made the experience transformative. I found a home in James. And I found a life-long interest in consciousness.

Here was a psychologist, trained in the scientific method, building a bridge between the long heritage of stories that are at the core of both science and religion.

Both disciplines, then and now, ask many of the same questions related to ultimate meanings, beginnings and endings, creation and death. Both are concerned with how life begins, how a single cell becomes a thinking human being and what happens to consciousness when we die. Nowhere is this more apparent than in the realm of consciousness, where there are times the storylines seem not only to converge but to embrace each other.

It is through consciousness that all personal experience, perception, belief, feelings, and action are filtered. What is deemed spiritual, the belief in a Divinity, the belief in an afterlife, the belief in the immortality of the soul, and the experience of Divine Presence also manifests in individual consciousness. And so the question that both science and theology explore is: What is consciousness and how does it work?

James was interested in all psychological phenomena not accounted for by normal consciousness that seemed to display "really supernormal knowledge." Although his major interest was mysticism, that state of consciousness described by those who have experienced it as "oneness with the universe" or "oneness with the Divine," his research included all realms of consciousness that, like mysticism, seemed to go beyond normal. This included all paranormal and psychic phenomenons. Among his areas of research were extra-sensory perception, psychokenesis (mind over matter), déjà vu, dreams, genius, automatic writing, hallucinations, mediumship, deathbed visions, and near-death experiences.

He wrote that a serious study of mysticism forces us to go beyond merely acknowledging that consciousness is real and needs to be explained. He concluded that mysticism, a sense of being one with the Divine, is a reality of a different order than anything else encountered in the empirical world. James suggested that these experiences are found on a continuum. They stretch upward from a rudimentary but related type of mysticism to a full mystical experience. At the rudimentary end of the spectrum, he writes of the significance that often attaches itself to a passage of music or poetry, the play of light, sound, a sense of déjà vu. Here also reside the borderline mystical states, awakened by scenes of great natural beauty, whose effect is beyond intellectual understanding and experienced as holy and manifesting a divine presence.

Finally, at the far end of the continuum of *presence* is a spontaneous mystical experience as described in the writing of saints and spiritual leaders. Others describe it as a "cosmic consciousness," that sense of being one with the universe.

The physicist Fritjof Capra wrote of one such personal experience in *The Tao of Physics*. He was sitting by the ocean, watching the waves and feeling the rhythm of his own breathing, when his awareness was suddenly transformed. "I 'saw' cascades of energy coming down from outer space, in which particles were created and destroyed in rhythmic pulses; I 'saw' the atoms of the elements and those of my body participating in this cosmic dance of energy; I felt its rhythm and I 'heard' its sound, and at this moment I knew . . ."

This experience is not unlike the visions of mystics, described throughout the centuries, long before the tools of science were capable of revealing to physicists the spin and charge of cosmic energy. This was long before science revealed the atoms of our bodies are traceable to the actions of stars that exploded those atoms into the galaxy out of which our solar system was formed. Writing in *Hemisphere Magazine*, the astrophysicist Neil De Grasse Tyson points out that this fact tells us "not only do we live in the universe, the universe lives within us."

Acknowledging Presence as a valid form of knowledge are the stunning words of a religious agnostic, Albert Einstein: ". . . that deeply emotional conviction of the Presence of a superior reasoning power is revealed in the incomprehensible universe—this forms my idea of God."

Like Einstein, it is that little phrase—"my idea of God"—that catches one's attention. Is that not all any of us have? An idea, which can't be proven or disproven. We are asked to attach our own image, either that prescribed by a religious institution or an image that spontaneously arises out of our own experience and consciousness.

James wrote of four characteristics shared by these experiences, from the rudimentary upwards. The first is ineffability, in that the mystical experience defies expression and must be experienced directly. It can't be transferred to another. The second characteristic is a noetic or knowing quality, a state of insight unplumbed by the intellect that carries a sense of authority for after-time. The third is transiency. A mystical experience, which is typically very intense, lasts a short period of time, anywhere from a few seconds to a few hours. The fourth characteristic is passivity, in that it can't be planned for but tends to break in upon and engulf the person as though originating from a region outside normal consciousness.

These four characteristics of mystical consciousness, present in a rudimentary form also shine through the stories of people who have had a coincidence or sign experience. Although they do not approach the power of a full mystical experience, they share to a lesser degree the numinous characteristics of the mystical consciousness.

James looked for and found the generic roots of spiritual experience across cultures. One of his principal conclusion states, *"the conscious person is continuous with a wider self . . ."* In attempting to illuminate this wider self, James refers to a subliminal consciousness, *". . . each of us is in reality an abiding physical entity far more extensive than he knows—an individuality which can never express itself completely through any corporeal manifestation."* It is within this region of consciousness where *". . . the preamble of all religion resides . . ."* and a spiritual world exists. This spiritual interior is each person's inheritance, the God within that manifests through what is highest and holiest in each person's consciousness. He suggested a continuum of consciousness into which *"minds can plunge as into a mother-sea or reservoir."*

There are sentences that shine on a page like gold nuggets in a mountain stream. And so it was for me when I first read

James's metaphor depicting consciousness as existing on a continuum that extended outside the body. The poetry of the phrase drew me in. It touched a chord within me, although, as a literal experience, it was beyond my imaginings.

Yet the idea of something grand and unseen existing beyond my brain, beyond everyone's brain, regardless of IQ or genius, resonated with me. James was alluding to something beyond experience, beyond the five senses, which I, and every other human being, is capable of accessing.

This was a new paradigm for me, a fresh way of perceiving the world. It brought with it an increased sensitivity for observing extraordinary moments of consciousness that arose like church spires above the landscape of the ordinary.

I read, re-read, highlighted and annotated my copy of James's book until it literally fell apart. I often kept a section at a time in my purse, along with apple juice and Band Aids for the kids. I would pull it out when waiting in line at the motor vehicle bureau or waiting for one of the kids to emerge from basketball practice on a fall afternoon.

The sense of Presence I read about in James held echoes of my own experience in the recovery room during the hours my infant was dying. It inflamed in me a desire to pursue this spiritual reality, this "more."

FOR CENTURIES WE have recorded our sense of the sacred through the presence of immensity. Who amongst us has not felt the presence of *something more* in the sheer majesty of the Grand Canyon or in images sent back from outer space of exploding stars and multiple galaxies? I have recently begun to wonder if the thrust toward travel is not on some level fulfilling a spiritual yearning. Perhaps modern travel is a form of pilgrimage, to refresh and nourish a spirit that has been depleted by living in the modern world. What is the kinship we feel with those who lived centuries ago and carried the massive stones to the altars of Stonehenge and to the tombs of the pyramids? With what do we resonate as we enter ancient temples in Indonesia that people built to appease or honor their gods? What gets opened up in us and filled when we visit a glacier in Alaska or stand beneath a waterfall in Costa Rica or witness a herd of elephants on the plains of Africa? Does this immensity not stun us into the kind of silence to which the poet Mary Oliver refers to as that "in which another voice may speak"?

When I read this, I was catapulted back to my twelve-year-old self. Freezing rain had bequeathed sleeves of ice to every branch, twig, stem, and bush that stood dormant alongside miles of New Jersey roadways. I was riding in a car with my father as the sun burst through the gray winter clouds and transformed the thousands of skeleton trees into crystal. It was like seeing the woods for the first time and hearing the intricate network of branches singing, the cells of my body with them. On another occasion it was the wonder of a tiny foot felt through my maternity dress and my skin as my child made himself known to me.

What James offered me was captured in the following sentences, for which I am forever grateful. "For practical life at any rate, the *chance* of salvation is enough. No fact in human nature is more characteristic than its willingness to live on a chance. The existence of the chance makes the difference . . . between a life in which the keynote is resignation and a life in which the keynote is hope."

This simple sentence was the one I was looking for. It spoke directly to my doubts. It offered me a choice. I could choose to live in the possibility—or not. *Salvation* was James's word. I translated it to encompass what salvation meant to me. I was looking for my child and, by extension, every mother's child.

Believing in chance allowed me to hope. Even though doubt was a weed that would insist on flourishing, chance was the keynote in a fragile faith.

Chapter 5

Stories That Changed the World in Religion and Science

"We tell ourselves stories in order to live."

Joan Didion

A s I LIVED MY OWN STORIES and gathered others, I became more and more aware that it is in hearing the stories of another's experience that we become open to new possibilities. It is personal experience that fuels the engine of stories. We have many abstractions in our language: justice, love, jealousy, peace, hope, and desire, to name a few. Standing alone, without a story, the words are hollow. But once you attach the story, the abstraction comes alive. You hear a man is very kind. Then you hear the story of how he gave up his kidney for a stranger. Now you really understand kindness.

A story's destination in the outer world is incalculable. No one knows where it may go to do its work. I think of Alcoholics Anonymous, which some have called the greatest spiritual movement of the twentieth century. It posits no specific religion or god but relies on the acknowledgement of a higher power, that is, something beyond oneself. It is structured around people telling their stories while others listen. The listener is simply asked to withhold judgment and to identify with the speaker or storyteller when aspects of the story resonate with his or her own experience. It is the story that holds the power to change lives.

This truth was hammered home to me in my work as a psychotherapist and later in the stories I collected for this book. Loss often precipitates the emotion that sends someone to therapy. Yet the stories behind the loss, the personal experiences that someone unravels and unknots are as diverse as leaves on a tree. Each story holds a different key to understanding and change.

The origin of a story lies in the inner world of the narrator. It is the map of what the poet might call another person's personal landscape, what the philosopher would call another's truth, and the scientist might identify as another's consciousness. Just as reading the stories of other's spiritual experience in William James validated my own experience in the recovery room after John's birth, the stories of religion and science serve as the underpinnings of what we believe and what we don't. The story seeps into the consciousness of the listener, who extracts meaning from it whether he accepts or rejects it.

There is evidence from the long tradition of worship that men and women have always intuited a larger reality, a spiritual reality. It has been called by many names, among them Heaven, Nirvana, Eternity, Immortality, and Spirit World. Sacred stories of Muslim, Jewish, Buddhist, and Christian heritage, and every other spiritual tradition, were born out of the evolving consciousness of the human race and translated into stories, long before science had the tools to examine them.

The stories reflect the intuition that unseen forces influence lives. In a very real sense, religion emerged with tools and fire. It served to name the sacred and invisible power that created life and took life. In every culture known (by last count over four thousand societies), a spiritual tradition developed to wrestle with questions that have plagued human beings since consciousness first erupted. Yearning to understand is part of the human condition. To ask *why* is ingrained in the psyche at birth.

From the rituals of primitive tribes through the myths of ancient civilizations, through folklore and legend and culminating in the written words of the world's great religious texts, it is the story that records the wisdom.

Science also moves forward through stories. The explosion in scientific knowledge that took place in the twentieth century is offering new ways to approach the intuitions about beginnings and endings, about life and death.

Although theories of a round earth existed since the time of Pythagoras in the sixth centry B.C., it wasn't until Columbus landed on the shores of the Americas that the story of a flat world finally dissolved. When Galileo demonstrated that the earth revolved around the sun, the narrative of earth and man being the center of the universe changed. In the four hundred years since Galileo, science has uncovered a universe so vast as to be unfathomable.

Before Darwin, the concept of evolution was still hidden. His discoveries led to a new paradigm of how humans and human consciousness came into existence.

Before the twentieth century it was undisputed that the universe was perceived to be a vast and fixed place, a celestial container that housed the stars and planets and everything else. On November 22, 1914, the first winds of change whispered a new story. Albert Einstein created his general theory of relativity, extending his special theory of relativity to include the idea that the universe was expanding in all directions. He, like every other scientist at work for the prior three hundred years, had assumed the universe was an unchanging infinite space. If this expanding idea was true, it would shatter the worldview of everyone, himself included.

According to accepted science, Einstein made the discovery but abandoned it shortly afterwards because it was incomprehensible to him. Believing he made a mistake, he reworked his equations. He added a mathematical term called the "cosmological constant," and adjusted his equations to fit with the prevailing worldview of the universe as being unchanging infinite space. It wasn't until some time in the 1920s, when Einstein visited the laboratory at Mount Palomar and saw for himself through the powerful Hubble telescope that galaxies were expanding away from each other and us, did he acknowledge that his original equations were, in fact true. He called his adjustment "the greatest blunder of my scientific career."

The implications were monumental. An expanding universe meant that the universe had a birthplace, a center in space, an edge to its existence, which was the beginning point of time. The Big Bang theory entered history.

Elizabeth Johnson, CSJ, a theologian, writes in *Ask the Beasts, Darwin and the God of Love*, about the stories of religion that have had to change in order to accommodate the complex discoveries of science. For example, the image of heaven as a place "above," a dome covering the earth, no longer fits the religious imagination. Nor does the biblical book of Genesis, which limits God's creation of the world and everything in it to a six-day period of historical time. The scientific evidence proves otherwise, seemingly pulling religion and science apart. Johnson demonstrates how the Genesis story and others can be understood as religious mythic narrative, the intent of which is to teach underlying truths and convey ultimate meanings about the God humans have always intuited.

AS I WRITE THESE WORDS, it is the eighteenth day of the search for the Malaysian airplane believed to have gone down somewhere within an 18,000-mile radius in the Indian Ocean. Two hundred and seven people have vanished. They leave family, friends, and business associates and the world stunned by their sudden and incomprehensible absence. I can't help but wonder if in the years to come individual stories will emerge from those left behind that speak to a retrospective anticipation of the tragedy by either those who lost their lives or those left to mourn them. Perhaps this will take the form of a sense of foreboding, a sign, a message, a vision presenting itself in the consciousness of someone associated with the tragedy.

This is not unheard of. A stunning book, *Messages, Sign, Visits and Premonitions from Loved Ones Lost on 9/11*, contains interviews with survivors of those lost on September 11, 2001, the day two planes crashed into the World Trade Center in New York City. The author, Bonnie Mc Enereny, narrates her own true story and those of countless others whom she interviewed. Each told of extraordinary events, unexplainable by natural law, interpreted as a sign from loved ones who lost their lives that day.

Compellingly, she tells of her husband's foreboding and terror in the days prior to the planes crashing into the towers, his reluctance to board the train and travel to Manhattan from Connecticut, and her own sign from him four days after the tragedy, when she felt his presence and he communicated his death to her. As friends and relatives gathered inside the house to keep a vigil with her, she left and went into the backyard. Alone with her terror-riddled thoughts, she stood gazing at the beautiful, natural-stone wall surrounding their property that her husband had put his heart and soul and love into building. She writes, "Everything around me was still—not a ripple in the air. Then all of a sudden, somewhere above me, I heard the beginning of a rush of a gust of new wind building up in intensity . . . I could see the wind! It created such a strong pattern through the leaves and the trees that it was easy to follow. . . . Then just as suddenly as it started, it stopped. I knew my question about his survival had been answered. 'He's gone,' I thought. 'It's over.'"

In each case chronicled by McEnereny, in a spontaneous uprush of consciousness, something seemingly unknowable was known. These intensely personal experiences, replete with personal meaning, were integrated as signs to the survivors. As with the stories included in these pages, the communication imbedded in the experience was conveyed through discrete, idiosyncratic, intimate information, whose content had its origins in the shared history between the living and the lost.

For some the experience was interpreted as a sign of post-mortem survival, defined in the scientific literature as the persistence of elements of mind and personality following bodily death. For the secular community, such an experience is integrated as a comfort and an aid to grieving. For those in the faith community, an extension of this experience is a validation of their already held belief in God and a belief in life after death.

These stories all include moments of Presence, a brush with something "more" that touched on the sacred. The experience spoke to a sense of immortality, as a sign of post-mortem survival manifesting itself to the narrator. Science and religion converge as ordinary people experience what seems beyond the natural order, a glimmering of infinity. This is what I believe the author Christian Wiman depicts when he writes, "to feel one's ultimate existence within one's daily existence."

Einstein, who translated mathematical formulas into stories that changed the world, wrote, ". . . the only truth is personal experience." The scientist, Rupert Sheldrake, writing in *The Sun*, amplified this view when he spoke about ". . . the need for every science to be empirical, which means 'based on experience.' Every science has to start from natural history, which involves describing what we perceive with our senses." He illustrates his point about the value of personal stories, even in science, with Darwin's *The Variation of Animals and Plants under Domestication* and *On the Origin of the Species*. In both books, acclaimed and accepted by the scientific community, there were very few lab experiments. Rather, Darwin collected anecdotal experiences from chicken breeders and rose growers and pigeon fanciers. He interviewed explorers and travelers who gave reports from different parts of the world. He compiled his information by talking to men and women about what they observed and experienced. The natural history preceded the scientific experimentation. That would come later.

Shelldrake collects stories in areas of telepathy and extra-sensory perception. These stories go to the heart of consciousness as they demonstrate an expanded ability to access information unaccountable by any of the current laws of science. He acknowledges that one or two anecdotes don't tell you a lot, but if you have hundreds of anecdotal stories of people saying largely the same thing, independent of each other, it tells you something.

That "something" may be that incidents of consciousness seeming to defy natural law will eventually be explained by science. Yet what I learned in the years that followed was that scientific discoveries were beginning to support a view challenging the scientific dogma, prompting many scientists to join with theologians who find a belief in science compatible with a belief in a God beyond our imagining.

Chapter 6

The Search Begins
1970

"I go . . . to forge in the smithy of my soul the uncreated consciousness of my race."
                                                            James Joyce

L ATER, A CHANCE ENCOUNTER with another book led me to other kinds of presence that echoed immortality and to the coincidence stories presented in the following pages. The stories in turn led me to theologians and scientists who continue to build the bridge between the two disciplines as they attempt to answer the questions about beginnings and endings, life and death.

In 1972, as I leafed through the newspaper, my attention was riveted by a book review of *The Search for a Soul*, a biography of the mid-twentieth-century author Taylor Caldwell, written by Jesse Stern. The title drew me in. It resonated with my search for my infant son. It alluded to my constant thoughts about John that I guarded obsessively, lest he be erased and eradicated from my world. Did he exist at all outside my thoughts?

Taylor Caldwell was a prolific author of over twenty novels. She was often mystified by the vast reservoir of detailed knowledge of medieval centuries that seemed to flow automatically from a source deep within her and into her writing as her novels unfolded. She spurned the idea suggested by others that she was gifted with psychic ability or that reincarnation was the wellspring of her knowledge. She accounted for the phenomena of her automatic writing by attributing her abilities to genetic memory, passed on through the cells of her body. She compared herself to "the fledging swallows taking the same course south as their ancestors, or the salmon and sea turtles journeying thousands of miles to the spawning grounds of their forbearers."

She adamantly rejected reincarnation, as proposed by others. She claimed to yearn for oblivion after death. She told her biographer, Jess Stern, that her husband of forty years, Marcus, had never believed in an afterlife either. They talked about it often and Marcus had once said, ". . . if there is life after death, I will come back and give you a sign."

On the day before her husband died, their gardener suggested that a shrub of resurrection lilies be dug up and replaced with something more productive. The plant had not bloomed in the twenty-one years since it was planted in the yard. Caldwell refused the gardener's offer. She had not been in the mood for gardening and, besides, she had a sentimental affection for the shrub. It had given her and Marcus many a laugh over the years. He had often joked, "You can't prove the resurrection by these lilies."

Marcus died on August 13, 1970. Paralyzed with grief, Taylor did not go to the wake or funeral but shut herself in her room, inconsolable. Dispite her professed belief previous to this, she desperately wanted to believe that death was not the end, if not for her, then for Marcus. Three days later, Taylor Caldwell reports being shaken to the core when her housekeeper excitedly called her to the window and pointed to the resurrection lily plant. "There was a blaze of white where the shrub had been bare the day before. Every bud had burst into glorious fragrance."

Struck by the sight, she asked herself, "Could this be the promised sign or was it coincidence?" The question is as valid today was it was in 1970. Although there could never be a verifiable answer as required by science, Taylor Caldwell found herself changed by the incident as an object of the material world manifested itself in such a way that it became symbolic of a deeper reality. It is the internal change brought about by personal experience that spoke to her, intimating there is indeed something more. It led her to the search documented in the book that had so captivated my interest.

Taylor Caldwell's story comforted me. I hung onto it, a little seed of possibility in the arid field of grief when I found myself imagining my dead child, talking to him. This was the child I carried in my heart if not in my arms, whose absence echoed in his brothers and sister riding their bicycles, sleeping in their beds. It reverberates still in the way his brief existence changed my life and the life of my family.

Search for a Soul opened a Pandora's box of questions I had not approached before. How did knowledge, manifested through her automatic writing, pour through her pen as she wrote her novels? Was it a form of psychic ability? Was it evidence of reincarnation? Was it a spiritual experience? Were there others who have similar experiences? What does this imply about consciousness? Is consciousness related to God?

In 1973, an event associated with the death of my husband's brother propelled a more personal interest in presence associated with death. It was still not my own experience—that would come later—but it moved me along in my interest in signs as they relate to death.

Part III

Gathering Stories

Chapter 7

Brothers
1973

M Y HUSBAND'S BROTHER, Bill, was his hero and his champion. Six years older than Bob and the firstborn of three boys, he was the buffer between their binge-drinking father and the havoc he wreaked upon the family. Bill was quick to share—his basketball, his clothes, his car, and even his meager money—with his younger brother. In the early years of my marriage, while we washed diapers and made formula, Bill partied. He was the free-spirited, handsome ex-Marine with a new girlfriend taking him out to dinner every Saturday night. I rarely if ever saw the side of him that would emerge in a letter he wrote to my oldest son, Robert.

May of 1969. The occasion was Robert's First Communion. The letter, profound and heartfelt, was beyond my son's seven-year-old comprehension. Yet the message was timeless and spoke to both Bob and me of everything we could want for our child and probably everything Bill would have wanted for his own child if a much-desired pregnancy ever happened. We were both moved by Bill's sharing a side of himself that we had never seen before, an opening into his inner life; to what he held dear. We decided to save the letter for when our son was old enough to appreciate and understand both its contents and the love that went into its composition. I put the letter back in its envelope and slipped it into a blue satin baby book, my safe-keeping place for precious things: a lock of my son's blonde baby hair, a record of his first step, first word, and all the history one tends to accumulate for a first child. I replaced the baby book in its original cream-colored cardboard box and put it back in the cedar chest where I stored it. Then I forgot about it as life resumed its busy pace.

And busy it was. On Thanksgiving Eve of 1972, after months of anticipation, the three children, Bob, and I traveled to Canada. By this time, the loss of John had led us to four-year-old Kurt and five-year-old Eddie, brothers who had been cleared for adoption and who would enhance each one of our lives in unimaginable ways.

At that time, Bill learned he had inoperable lung cancer. He knew he was dying and was never able to travel from Detroit to meet the boys. During a phone call he hopefully suggested to Bob, "They will replace me in your life." Although Bill wanted to believe his own words, they weren't true. He was irreplaceable. Six months later, Bill was dead.

His funeral was held in Detroit, and a month later there was a memorial service back East. Bob wanted to give a eulogy. Bereft and feeling at a loss for words, his mind composed and discarded as not good enough all the jumbled thoughts he had about his brother. As he was about to go out the door the evening of his appointment to meet with the priest to prepare the liturgy, he remembered the letter. Here were Bill's own words. What better way to eulogize him than with the powerful aspirations he wrote for his godson, which indirectly spoke so eloquently about the man who penned them?

"Do you know where that letter Bill wrote to Robert for his First Communion is?"

"Probably in Robert's baby book," I answered, knowing that was my place to store all precious and not-to-be-misplaced papers.

"Where do you keep the baby books?

"With the other children's books in the cedar chest in the front hall. They should be stacked on the bottom, left-hand side." Since we hadn't had Kurt and Eddie as babies, I knew he would find only three satin books, one pink, one yellow, and one blue. "His is the blue one," I said.

Bob dashed to the hallway and removed the few plants that struggled to stay alive on top of the chest in the sun-deprived hallway. He pushed the tiny circle of the lock inserted in the walnut wood. As the scent of cedar filled the hallway, the jammed contents of the chest sprung into view: stuffed animals, photo albums, kindergarten drawings, baby shoes, hand-knit sweaters Bob's mother had made for her grandchildren, the baptismal outfit made from my wedding gown, adoption mementoes from our trip to Canada to pick up our two youngest sons . . .

I was in the kitchen, clearing the table, organizing homework when Bob called me with excitement. "Come quick, you're not going to believe this," he said.

When I got to the front hall I saw lying on top of everything, impossible to miss in the center of the chest, the very page of Bill's letter from which Bob wanted to quote. No envelope, no second page. Call it chance, call it coincidence, call it synchronicity, call it sign, but it has to be called something.

Then on a second thought, doubting what had just happened, he asked, "Did you put it there?"

I hadn't.

"Listen." Stumbling through emotion, he read aloud the words Bill wrote to our son three years earlier, which more than confirmed Bob's intuition that he wanted to use it at the service:

"Today our prayer for you is that God make you
Big enough to admit honestly all your shortcomings,
Brilliant enough to accept flattery without it making you arrogant,
Tall enough to tower above deceit,
Strong enough to welcome criticism,
Compassionate enough to understand human frailties,
Wise enough to recognize your mistakes,
Humble enough to appreciate greatness,
Staunch enough to stand by your friends,
Human enough to be thoughtful of your neighbor, and
Righteous enough to be devoted to the love of God."

When he finished reading, we both got down on our knees to rummage through the chest to look for the envelope and the rest of the letter. We assumed the envelope and second page would also be lying loose amidst the stored items. Piece by piece, we unloaded the contents of the cedar chest onto the floor; no envelope, no second page. Finally we came to the three baby books neatly stacked in the bottom left-hand corner. Opening the box containing the blue one, we found tucked between its pages the envelope and second page, just where I remembered placing it three years earlier.

Bob later told me that in that first glimpse of the letter, something extraordinary happened to him. Logically, he knew a letter couldn't transport itself from one spot to another. Yet that one loose page was so much more than a piece of paper. It was a brotherly nudge, a pat on the back from Bill, the way he used to acknowledge Bob when he hit a home run or scored points in a basketball game. It was a communion with Bill, a reassurance that the bond of brothers continued. His rational mind knew Bill was dead, yet at the same time exquisitely present in the tiny vestibule.

To stumble upon transcendent meaning can be transformative and so it was for Bob and, to a lesser degree, me. As an observer, I was caught in an intricate web of meaning, but my husband was so much more than an observer. He was a participant in that his whole life was marked by the influence of his brother, who revealed himself three years earlier in the letter, and now, in his spirit. The experience felt sacred.

Chapter 8

Mentor and Friend
1975

*"Whatever you can do, or dream you can, begin it. Boldness
has genious, power, and magic in it."*   Goethe

ONE OF THE INSIGHTS I gained from my years in therapy
was the realization that the choices I made further precluded my ability to go to college. Actually, a college degree was never really on the horizon. Although my family was not
poor, tuition money was not a priority when there were three siblings to feed and clothe behind me. Only once, as a high school
senior, did I express to a friend my fantasy about going away to
college. Along with this confession was the foregone conclusion
that it was a dream, not to be taken seriously. Somehow I had
adopted the mindset that it was boys who really needed college,
and it would be my brother, four years younger, for whom my parents might be able to eke out the tuition.

After graduating from high school, I worked as a represen-
tative for the New York Telephone Company. The company had
a tuition program whereby a passing grade at a certified college
would generate a tuition reimbursement. At that time, St. John's
University had a few buildings in downtown Brooklyn, within
walking distance from my job. As I recall, some of the evening
classes actually took place in a corrugated tin Quonset hut-type
structure, hastily constructed in the fifties for returning veterans.

With my parents' encouragement, tuition reimbursement, and the proximity to my job, I enrolled in evening classes. I would leave the telephone company and walk to St. John's twice a week, attend class, and then take the subway home. My mother saved the evening meal on a plate, warmed it in the oven and sat with me while I finally ate my dinner around ten o'clock.

By the time I managed to accumulate some fifteen credits on a sparse transcript from St. John's, I had gained insight in therapy that foregoing college was less a lost opportunity and more a dream deferred. In 1970, I enrolled in an evening class at Caldwell College in what, in retrospect, was one of the best decisions of my life.

I rarely spoke in class. I sat in the back of the room scribbling in my notebook the words the professor uttered, using the shorthand I had learned at the telephone company to record the complaints and requests of the customers with whom I spoke. I selected my classes by how they would fit into the children's week night schedule. Only secondarily was I motivated by my level of interest in the subject matter of the course.

Not wanting to tamper with whatever alchemy was playing a part in my release from depression as I participated in therapy, I avoided any class offered by the psychology department. I resisted the impulse to get too close to the therapeutic process from an academic perspective or of trying to stay a step ahead of the psychologist who was artfully helping me help myself.

As chance would have it, I happened upon a literature class taught by one of the Dominican nuns who staffed the college. As she facilitated discussion around the literature we read, the very existential questions that so occupied me in the privacy of therapy were woven into the classroom through the filter of her intelligence and spirituality. Soon my priorities for choosing classes changed. Having her for a professor superseded the convenience of a particular night. This nun, Sister Elizabeth, would become my spiritual mentor and my friend.

We were close to the same age, she a brilliant professor of literature and I the housewife/student who had left Brooklyn like a thought behind and rushed from high school into marriage, children, and the myth of living happily ever after. There was no way of knowing that September evening, as I took a seat in the back of her classroom that she would give me the most precious gift one person can give to another.

An aura of austerity about her was reflected in the absence of noise in her presence. A hush fell over the classroom when she approached, as though it became a sacred place. She carried a slim black leather notebook and assorted works of literature that she stacked neatly on the gray metal desk. She rarely consulted the books and seemed able to draw from some internal reservoir whatever material she needed to support a perspective. Her movements were measured and economical, as if an excess of motion would subtract from her point. As she thrust her hands deep inside the pockets of her long white skirt, I imagined some enormous library, accessed by osmosis, buried in the folds of the wool. Her ideas lit up that autumn classroom like lanterns in a Japanese garden. She invited each student to immerse herself in worlds created by the literature.

Initially I was afraid of her. She had knowledge, and I had learned that knowledge was power that could be used against me. How she might exert that power was the subject of my private fantasies. What it came down to was this: she could find me out. I could not pretend in front of this woman. I believed she knew how much I didn't know; like a peeled orange, no longer able to hide behind the rind of motherhood, I was exposed in this class of "twenty-somethings" in all my ignorance. My instinct was to run and find a safe history class in which to hide. A more prevailing instinct drew me back, and each Wednesday evening I found myself settling into the back of her classroom, my thoughts fired like molten iron.

The following semester she taught a course in poetry writing. In my thirty-three years, I had only written one poem, the one to John. Through the experience of writing it, I had stumbled upon a way out of a labyrinth of loss in which I had become immersed. I wanted to know more.

The poet Elizabeth Bishop wrote, "The poet is in the poem in spite of every subterfuge." As I worked to discover the language and form to express myself in poetry, I lay open on the page things held deepest within me.

Always the professional, Sister Elizabeth guided my verbs, questioned my adjectives and considered my images with respect, while holding herself distant from any involvement in the emotional content of the writing or the life it reflected.

After graduation, as I continued to write, it was always her reaction I anticipated in my mind's eye. As I struggled to discover the right word or create the perfect metaphor, I envisioned her small, neat handwriting in the margins, the fine line of her ink pen, and her way of dotting the "i" with a tiny circle. She was my unseen and unseeing audience. With much trepidation, a year later I called her.

"Yes, of course I remember you. Come to my office with your poems," she said.

My palms were damp as I watched her read. She held each sheet of paper lightly in her hands as if any impression of her fingers would intrude on the poem. I saw no reaction on her face. She read the last page, carefully laid it down on her desk and looked at me. She did not say the poems were good, the words I yearned to hear. But what she did say caused a rush in my brain, the way I imagine cocaine must feel coursing through the brain of an addict.

"How nice it would be if you and I could work together as peers."

With those words, this extraordinary woman, who had sensed my admiration, relinquished the power I had bestowed upon her as the high priestess of knowledge. She gave that part of herself to me and invited me into her world.

It was she, Sister Elizabeth, who shared the following two personal stories that linked with my own interest in signs.

Chapter 9

Ray's Story
THE CHEMOTHERAPY ROOM

DURING THE COURSE of his treatment for cancer, Ray befriended a nine-year-old boy, Sean, who was also undergoing cancer treatment at the same hospital. They met in the chemotherapy waiting room where the only things thriving were the potted plants and the fish, swimming serenely in oversized tanks, A simple "Hi, what's your name?" between the freckle-faced boy and the seventy-five-year-old man evolved into an unlikely friendship. The nurses acquiesced to their request to share the same little room as the chemo released its long, slow drip into their bodies. Sitting side by side in their twin chairs, the older man's jokes and the boy's laughter spilled into the quiet cancer corridors and made passersby smile.

A time came when the boy was hospitalized as an inpatient, Ray, with the help of his wife, Anne, found his way to Sean's room on the pediatric floor every few days to visit his young friend. Sometimes Anne would protest, "You've got to get home and rest, Ray." But he would insist, "Sean's the best medicine for me."

Ray was doing well and still hoping for remission. His death while he slept one night was shocking and unexpected. Anne knew she had to tell Sean; the boy would be looking for his friend. But beyond that, she knew Ray would want Sean to know that his death wasn't scary. It didn't hurt, and Ray hadn't been scared.

With this in mind, Anne, accompanied by her oldest son, went to the hospital the following day to deliver the surprising news to Sean. She steeled herself to witness the boy's tears and to avoid breaking down herself.

But it was the boy who surprised her. She began, "I have something to tell you, Sean—" when Sean interrupted

"I already know," his voice floated from the cloud of white linens that covered his bed. "Ray died last night," he said.

Anne's first thought was that the medical staff, although she could not imagine how, had somehow become aware of Ray's death and told the boy before she arrived. She paused and said, "Yes, he died, Sean, but there are some things about Ray's death I think he would want you to know. That's why we came by."

"Yeah, I already know that, too. He visited and told me himself," Sean said.

Anne was flabbergasted and didn't know how to respond. She looked to Sean's nurse for help. The woman had a quizzical look on her face and shook her head from side to side as she mouthed, "We didn't tell him. We didn't even know."

Thinking the boy was mixed up and alluding to some previous conversation from one of Ray's visits, Anne asked, "When did he come by, Sean?"

"He came to see me right before you came. He sat right there on the edge of the bed, and he told me dying was easy. He told me not to be afraid. It doesn't hurt when you die. He said he'd be waiting for me. Then he smiled, got up and walked right out the door just as you were coming in. He passed right by you. Didn't you see him?"

"No, I didn't see him," she told Sean.

Anne knew there was no explaining Sean's experience, no logic that she or anyone else could decipher. Yet the question remained: How had the very words she so carefully prepared made themselves known in Sean's consciousness before she even spoke them? Anne didn't know. The nurse didn't know. But it didn't matter. Sean was unfazed, and that's what did matter. His visible joy at having experienced his friend's presence and message spread to Anne and to her son, as they stood by the bed witnessing this gift Ray had given to both of them through the dying boy.

This was a different kind of presence than Divine Presence, yet for Anne and her son and for those who later heard the story recounted at the funeral, it reverberated with a sense of something otherworldly, a sense of something holy that flirted with both theology and science.

My radar for stories of profound personal experiences that evoked transcendence remained on alert.

Chapter 10

Carol's Story
THE VISIT

C AROL WAS A NON-DENOMINATIONAL Christian who, after the birth of her two young children, found herself drawn to the Catholic Church. She began a course of study that would lead to baptism and she asked her surprised mother-in-law, Elizabeth, to be her godmother. Elizabeth was more than delighted. She stood proudly alongside Carol at the baptism as Carol's husband, Elizabeth's son, and the rest of the family witnessed Carol's welcome into the church. It was obvious an intimate spiritual connection existed between the two women, one that probably exceeded the typical mother/daughter-in-law relationship and perhaps had bearing on what followed. Two short years later, Elizabeth took sick and died.

In 1977, a full three years after Elizabeth's death, Carol was lying in bed one morning, anticipating the first stirrings from the children's room that would let her know her day was about to start. She opened her eyes to what she later described as a vision of Elizabeth sitting on the edge of her bed, as though waiting for her to acknowledge her presence. As Carol's mind registered the information, Elizabeth reached out and patted her hand in a gesture she internalized as . . . as she didn't know what.

Carol had a strong sense that her mother-in-law was trying to tell her something, but no words were spoken, nothing communicated, before the encounter ended. Yet Carol felt gifted. A spontaneous feeling of safety and closeness to Elizabeth blossomed within her as the loving role Elizabeth had played in her life was rekindled.

She immediately shook her husband awake and excitedly told him, "Your mother just visited me. She came to tell me something."

"You must have been dreaming," he said groggily. And then laughingly, "or drinking. Mom's been dead for three years."

Carol knew she sounded unhinged. "No, really, she was sitting on the edge of the bed stroking my hand. She wanted me to know something."

"Oh, yeah? What did she want you to know?" he asked, still in a joking mode.

"I don't know. It was vague, but I know she was here in this room, as real as you are right now. I felt her touch my hand."

Her husband continued to doubt. "She's my mother, why would she be visiting you and not me?" he joked as he attempted to dismiss or dissuade his wife from her brief leave-taking from reality.

Carol refused to be put off, convinced of what she had encountered.

All that day, she went about her regular routine, getting the kids off to school, straightening the house, doing laundry, shopping for groceries, making dinner. Yet the experience followed her the way an echo rumbles through a canyon. As the hours went by and distanced her from the immediacy of the experience, she began to doubt herself.

She asked herself, *Was it a dream? Should I believe my own intuition that's telling me it's so much more?* All day she was shadowed by the need to know what her mother-in-law was trying to tell her. No amount of rational thought allowed her to figure it out. She was still preoccupied that evening when the phone rang as she stood at the sink rinsing the dinner dishes. She turned off the faucet, removed her hands from the water and picked up the phone. In the moments that followed, Carol's world collapsed— and at the same time crystallized. Like a negative developing in a darkroom, a fully formed picture of her encounter with Elizabeth grew inside her as she listened to her own mother's sobbing voice on the other end of the line.

"There's been a car accident, a terrible accident."

Carol's nineteen-year-old brother had been killed on his way home that evening.

What had so preoccupied her all day was suddenly illuminated as the light that was her brother was extinguished. Stunned by sorrow as she absorbed this new reality, Carol was grasped by the knowledge that the encounter with her mother-in-law that morning had preceded her brother's death by almost twelve hours. Her heart leapt in all its newly broken pieces with an understanding that was beyond understanding. Along with the grief that overwhelmed her, her consciousness absorbed a consoling belief that her brother was not alone in that wrecked automobile as he took his last breath. By extension, he was not alone now.

But Carol's story didn't end there. Three years later, for the second and final time, Carol experienced her mother-in-law's presence. Again she awakened to Elizabeth sitting on the edge of the bed and wordlessly trying to tell her something. This time Carol was terrified. She was pregnant. A thought shot through her like electricity: *Elizabeth has come again to warn me. I'm going to lose this baby just like I lost my brother.*

Frantically, she spread her palms over her abdomen and felt for stirrings in her womb, willing her unborn child to kick or move. She awakened her husband. "It happened again. Your mother came to me again. Just like the last time. She's warning me. I'm going to lose the baby!" He tried to calm her, as did the doctor when she saw him later that day. But secretly, her husband was scared, too.

In this world of cause and effect, past experience is the accepted predictor of future behavior. The tragic aftermath of her mother-in-law's presence in the hours that preceded her brother's death, that morning three years earlier, was written in her bones in a terrifying and foreboding language.

As I listened to Sister Elizabeth tell me of her sister-in-law's experience, I identified with Carol's fear. I held my breath for the story to be completed. I, too, feared she would lose the baby. But no, no tragedy befell her. Two weeks later, she gave birth without any complications to her third child, a healthy son.

I found myself returning over and over to this second encounter. Although I never experienced the presence of the dead visiting me in the vivid way Carol had, I have occasionally been terrified by night dreams pushing their way into my day and taunting me with presentiments of tragedy. When a dream pursued me with intimations of something awful happening to someone I loved, I thought of Carol and the anguish she felt as she projected a tragedy that never materialized. And I would calm.

What Carol's story left with me was the folly of trying to interpret such experiences definitively. Her second, benign experience allowed me to dispense with torturing myself with frightening meanings created in my own imagination. In both instances she was unable to figure out, let alone control the experience. Whether vision or dream, one precluded tragedy; the other did not. Yet the common thread woven through both incidents was a manifestation in Carol's consciousness that Elizabeth, like a guardian angel, continued in some unknowable dimension. And by extension, so did her brother.

As I accumulated these stories, I could not help wonder how such encounters entered consciousness. What, if anything, could they tell us about death and afterlife? Living the questions excited me and gave me hope.

Part IV

Scholarship

Chapter 11

The Dawning of a New Awareness
1979

"Without the slightest doubt there is something through which material and spiritual energy hold together and are complementary . . . in the last analysis . . . there must be a single energy operating in the world." Pierre Teilhard de Chardin

A S THE SEVENTIES PROGRESSED, clinical depression no longer held me hostage. We had adopted our two youngest sons in 1972, and life was busy with the hustle and bustle of five children. William James's prescription to "live on chance" was my "go to" action when the existential questions about God, an afterlife, and the ultimate meaning of life that culminates in death threatened to take me down again. And, always, there was the undertow of my encounter in the recovery room after John's birth, when the memory of my personal experience of God's presence pulled me back into an eddy of its light. Although the immediacy and power of the experience diminished with time, the memory served as a touchstone to return to again and again. It had happened and even doubt could not make it un-happen.

And yet as the scientific revolution advanced, the underpinnings of long-held beliefs continued to be challenged by an ever-increasing body of scientific evidence. Four centuries ago, astronomy and the mathematical equations of Galileo confirmed the Earth was not the center of the universe. Although we may have accepted Galileo's evidence, a map of the universe was not available to us. In 1969, Apollo 10 astronauts landed on the moon and witnessed the earth rising above its horizon. Television and newspapers captured it in pictures and *Earthrise* contributed to a new world consciousness. The Apollo moon landing images confirmed for everyone that heaven was no longer "up there" and earth "down here." The earth is in heaven. No longer divided, they are one. There is a unity in the universe. There is no division.

Science had already refuted the creation story of Genesis as evidence of the Big Bang became mainstream. Biblical stories I held dear since childhood were thrown into question. Noah and his ark, Jonah in the belly of the whale, or even Adam and Eve and the forbidden apple were relegated to myth.

These stories gradually transformed themselves into individual shards of glass poking holes in the blind faith of my childhood. If the bedrock of the Old Testament were no longer believable, what did that say about Jesus and the New Testament? What did that say about God?

Around this time, Sister Elizabeth offered a seminar class in mythology. I enrolled. As autumn drifted into winter, ten of us gathered around a carved mahogany conference table for four hours on consecutive Saturday mornings. Here I first grappled with the concept of the Old Testament as myth, that is, stories not literally true, but created to illustrate an underlying truth; stories as symbol.

Myths with common underlying themes about creation, virgin births, incarnation, death, resurrection, second comings, and judgment day that arose in diverse cultures throughout recorded time were laid out before me. In some sense I found this shattering. I did not want to know that the sacred stories of my religion had their roots in religions that preceded it. I didn't want to know that myths of virgin birth like Osiris, an ancient god of Egypt, and Mithra, a Persian sun god, persisted in over thirty-two religious traditions, some preceding Christianity by three thousand years. I didn't want to know that the reliability of a single religious group, my group, possessing an exclusive truth couldn't be sustained.

In the discussions in this seminar, my Catholic provincialism broke down. I came to recognize the common search for God that myth reflected since humans began telling stories to explain truths for which there was no objective evidence.

What was most compelling to me was that each of the thousands of myths, derived from thousands of cultures and preserved through generations, came through each individual's consciousness. Divergent people separated by geography and time had reached similar conclusions to acknowledge a supreme God. With this came the unfolding realization that the sacred was accessible to all. This reinforced for me that consciousness, as suggested by William James, was indeed a portal to the divine.

Delving into mythology moved me forward in understanding the universality of humanity's search for God. Yet it also created an overwhelming sense of loss. Things were not as they seemed. More questions than answers arose in my personal quest for God, who had been so near in the person of Jesus Christ in the Catholic classrooms of my youth.

In April of 1979, *The New York Times* printed an interview with Joseph Campbell, a world-renowned expert on religion and mythology. When Campbell was asked how he would define mythology, he answered, "Other peoples' religion." I could so relate. I realized I was one of those who off-handedly rejected, and thus didn't pursue the sacred texts that supported other faiths. Believing I had the truth, which emanated from the unquestioning faith of my childhood, I had built a wall around my religion believing there was no need to go further.

When asked his definition of religion, Campbell answered, "Misunderstanding mythology." He elaborated on how misunderstanding comes from reading spiritual mythological symbols as though they were references to historical events. Campbell referred to myth as a mask of God, a metaphor for what lies behind the visible world. However, the mystic or spiritual traditions differ, both in the past and in the present; they all share in calling an individual to a deeper awareness, a deeper consciousness.

Campbell's words took some of the sting out of my new-found knowledge.

Yet it wasn't easy to relinquish what I had always perceived as the truth. It was even harder to discover the way to reconcile that loss.

During those years, Joseph Campbell was introduced into the mainstream consciousness by Bill Moyers, who produced a multi-series television interview, followed by a book with him. That book, *The Power of Myth*, became the axis of a group of ten of my Jewish acquaintances who became close friends through the discussions that ensued. Over the course of eighteen months we hauled bread, fruit, cheese, and our individual copies of *The Power of Myth* to each other's homes one Saturday night a month to discuss myth and how our individual religious heritages integrated it. One year I was honored by an invitation to play a role in the Passover supper. Through that sacred ritual, I actually experienced the bond between the Old Testament and the New. On another occasion, I took out my crystal rosary beads and answered one of the several in the group's questions about the rosary, a tradition that was so much a part of my heritage.

All this while, as I confronted and came to appreciate others' faith, I continued to live on the chance prescribed by William James that all the questions were leading me somewhere.

One winter Sunday after packing the five protesting children off to Mass, I came across a slim book stacked in a metal rack in the vestibule of the church along with pamphlets on the lives of the saints and flyers on potluck dinners and Bingo. It was called *How I Believe* and was written by a French Jesuit priest, Teilhard de Chardin. The title drew me in. *How I Believe.* Perhaps this man could pull me back into the fold, where it was comfortable and secure.

I put my two-dollar offering into the receptacle to purchase the book and had my first exposure to the man whose words dovetailed with both those of William James and Joseph Campbell. Teilhard would propel the direction of religious thought for generations to come as his views incorporated science into the understanding of God.

Here was my first exposure to the theologian who was both a scientist and a mystic, and whose work culminated in a belief in a spiritual evolution of the universe. Based on his work as a scientist, he wrote of a constant drive toward higher degrees of complexity in evolution, moving toward a culmination in what he referred to as the Omega Point—the evolution and integration of all personal consciousness where all would be drawn together as one in a "world soul."

He wrote of salvation for all people for all time.

I can't say I comprehended this at the time. Yet to find a Catholic theologian embracing the inclusiveness implicit in a "world soul" and "Cosmic Christ" was more than inviting and echoed the explanations around myth. Some instinct prompted me to save the book.

Many years later I found that paperback squeezed between more hefty books on my bookshelf. Its pages had turned sepia with age, its spine cracked, but the words I had highlighted in yellow still illuminated the pages. Only then did I read the note that preceded the foreword. The original work, from which Harper and Row published the slim little book in 1969, had been written in 1934. It remained unpublished for the next thirty-five years, during which time the Catholic Church banned Teilhard's writings. Forbidden from publishing or teaching, he was often in exile, sent away by Church authorities and his Jesuit superiors because his views, which often diverged from "official" teachings of the Church, were considered dangerous to the laity. Trained as a paleontologist and a geologist, Teilhard was also known as a philosopher and a mystic. He took part in the discoveries of Peking man while in exile, even as he continued to write and develop his theology.

Only after his death in 1955 did Teilhard's works find their way into print. *The Divine Milieu*, written in 1927, was finally published in 1968 and the *Phenomenon of Man*, written in 1940, was published in 1959. These now-classic writings transformed future generations. A new breed of theologian emerged, one that further developed his work on the evolution of consciousness and incorporated it with the astonishing discoveries of quantum science.

On the first page of *How I Believe,* Teilhard wrote four simple but powerful declarative sentences:

> "I believe that the universe is an evolution.
> I believe that evolution proceeds toward spirit.
> I believe the spirit is fully realized in a form of personality.
> I believe that the supremely personal is the Universal Christ."

That second sentence captured my imagination: "*I believe that evolution proceeds toward spirit.*" It propelled me to seek that elusive thread of spirit that evolved from the cosmic soup of creation into human consciousness.

Teilhard believed that, along with the physical aspect of matter science explores, it was crucial to acknowledge a psychic or spiritual aspect of the cosmos. For Teilhard, evolution was not just about the realm of matter that encompasses everything that exists, including our bodies and our brains, all of which can be weighed and measured and ultimately examined. It was also about the realm of consciousness, the realm of spiritual energy, which can't be weighed or measured or held in one's hand, but exists nonetheless.

He referred to this as the *Within* of things, enclosed from the beginning of time within the stuff of the cosmos and the early earth. He saw this *Within* as co-extensive with a *Without*, which alone was measured by science. He held that the exterior world must inevitably be lined at every point with an interior one.

For Teilhard, as evolution unfolded it was the psychic aspect, the *Within*, that would become more prominent and lead to an Omega or end point in creation. Here all matter would become transformed into spiritual energy. He wrote, "Concretely speaking there is no matter and spirit: rather there exists only matter that is becoming spirit. The stuff of the universe is Spirit-Matter."

This resonated with me. What it said to me is the matter or stuff that is my body and the matter or stuff of your body has within it the potential to evolve to spirit. It allowed for an evolution leading to a kind of personal immortality for all people that survives the death of the body.

During the years I studied psychology I learned that psychological truths, those emanating from the psyche, are as valid as physical truths, which are limited to matter and alone are experienced as reality. Who can deny the existence of truth, beauty, or justice? Although they are abstractions, amorphous as air, we know them when we experience them and can distinguish one from the other as well as we can distinguish a face from a hand. Take grief—we know it intimately when it settles upon us even though it can't be weighed like a pound of potatoes or tossed away like an unwanted chair. This was brought home to me in a powerful way the day I witnessed the grief of a friend as she stood alongside the coffin of her son. The impulse to write a poem revealed to me something I didn't know I knew. It reflected what I was observing about the psychic truth of sorrow. Here is an excerpt about grief taken from that poem.

> it cannot be measured
> the way loss enters the body
> infusing it with pain so exquisite
> it is crushing under its weight
> and yet
> it weighs nothing

Mystics and mythmakers allude to an invisible world. Now Teilhard, a theologian who was also a scientist, was also alluding to the invisible world of consciousness.

Since the latter half of the twentieth century, consciousness—that place that is not a place, where we experience the Sacred and the Divine—where we experience God—has blossomed as an area of scientific study. It seems that even Einstein would have supported this, having written in his book, *The World as I See It,* "religious geniuses of all ages have been distinguished by this kind of cosmic religious feeling . . . In my view it is the most important function of art and science to awaken this feeling and keep it alive in those who are capable of it . . . I maintain that cosmic religious feeling is the strongest and noblest incitement to scientific research."

Although there is no record of theTeilhard and Einstein meeting, they were contemporaries. Teilhard was born in 1881, two years after Einstein. Both died in the United States, their adopted country, in April 1955, eight days apart, Einstein in Princeton, New Jersey, and Teilhard in New York, fifty miles away.

Both men based their life's work on understanding the unity behind all of creation. Constructing a beautiful metaphor capturing evolution of the universe since the Big Bang, Teilhard wrote, "The stars are laboratories in which the evolution of matter proceeds . . ."

To paraphrase Elizabeth Johnson, CSJ, science has demonstrated that out of the Big Bang came over 100 billion galaxies, each with over 100 billion stars; out of stardust came the Earth and out of the molecules of the Earth, life; out of life, consciousness, self-reflexive thought, and love, which is the ultimate flowering of those deep cosmic energies. Cosmic history demonstrates that everything is connected with everything else. Nothing exists on its own.

It was during a visit to the Hayden Planetarium in New York that the magnitude of this timeline was brought home to me in a visceral way. A model spanning the number of years between the Big Bang to the evolution of life, consciousness, and finally spirit is stunning. If the Big Bang was on January first, then our sun and planets came into existence September tenth and humans came on the scene December thirty-first at 11:50 p.m.

My initial exposure to Teilhard was my link to the works of other twenty- and twenty-first-century theologians and scientists. They have continued to develop and integrate his thoughts about a continuing evolution of spirit that survives the death of the body.

Today, those following and interpreting the work of Teilhard, writing on the website "Teilhard for Beginners, *The Divine Milieu* Explained," state, "Christ today is not just Jesus of Nazareth, raised from the dead, but rather a huge, continually evolving Being, as big as the universe. In this colossal, almost unimaginable

Being each of us lives and develops in a consciousness, like living cells in a huge organism."

For my purposes and the purposes of this book, it is the evolution of consciousness from the quantum vacuum that is so enticing. For it is within individual consciousness that we experience the cosmic religious feeling about which Einstein wrote. It is within individual consciousness that we experience divine presence about which the mystics wrote. It is within individual consciousness that we experience God, about which people have been writing since human thought first evolved out of that laboratory of the stars.

Part V

Consciousness

Chapter 12

Nanny's Story
1985

I N 1985, AN EVENT took place around the death of Nanny, my mother-in-law. It left me breathless and imprinted me with my own personal story, one that dovetailed with my intuition that there are signs that something unnamable survives death.

Death took its time with Nanny. I hardly noticed how it stalked her until the day she called to say there were children running around her apartment. There was no convincing her that she was alone, just imagining children on the back stairs who were finding their way through the locked door while she was asleep.

"They hide my purse and steal my money," she said.

As she listened to my explanation, her agitation escalated. When she sensed her efforts to convince me failed, she simply said, "So, you don't believe me."

"Yes, of course I believe you," I assured her as I broke my own rule and lied to my mother-in-law. Then, appealing to a logic I refused to believe was gone from this woman who taught me so much, most precious of which was how to be a mother-in-law, I said, "But it's impossible. See the bolt on the door?" I made my way to her hiding places and retrieved her purse. "Look, here's your wallet and your money. It was in the drawer with the silverware all the time."

She paused. I thought I had reached that fading part of her mind that was trying to reconstruct a world long gone. But, no, with renewed firmness she looked me straight in the eye and said, "The children put it there."

For the next three years, the slow, steady decline that would culminate in her refusal to eat ravaged her mind and body like some hungry bear released from its winter den. Foraging in the green forest of her intellect, it snapped each bud of a thought and gathered her words like a cache of almonds and hid them. Her flesh was picked clean and her dignity trampled.

One year later we made the decision for her to give up her tiny apartment and enter a nursing home. Sorting through the accumulations of a lifetime, I knew she would not be coming back.

I gathered a few things, the last remnants of her eighty years on this earth, to take with me. Foremost was her favorite dress, the one she wore to her surprise seventieth birthday party that she confessed was her first birthday party ever. It was fuchsia pink, and she had worn it only that one time. I took the American flag four Marines had snapped into a three-cornered triangle and placed in a clear vinyl case. It had remained untouched, swathed in tissue paper in the top drawer of her dresser, since the day thirteen years earlier when she stood stoic at the foot of her firstborn son, Bill's, casket to receive it. I gathered a wilted ivy plant that sat on top of her television, it's soil baked to hardpan, its few leaves brittle and browning.

I hung the fuchsia dress, sealed in its plastic bag, in the back of my closet for the inevitable day when we would need it. Thinking I might be able to revive the ivy, I placed it on a sunny window ledge in my family room next to a Christmas cactus she gave me years ago. Although the cactus never bloomed, its thick, green, shiny leaves grew so abundant I had re-potted it once or twice. I enjoyed the fact that it was a gift from Nanny that prospered even if she hadn't. I put the flag in the cedar hope chest, now stored in the attic.

EARLY ONE JANUARY MORNING about a year later, a call from the nursing home: come quickly. Finally, the long good-bye was over. I looked at her naked face, stripped of the pride she wore over the years. Confined between the bars of her crib-like bed, she was surrounded by very little she could call her own. A few photographs were propped up on the window sill alongside the philodendron turning brown from the draft.The blanket her sister crocheted, folded on the bedside chair, and her rosary beads wrapped around the bars of the bed may or may not have given her comfort. Here lay the pale shell of a woman whose fragile frame belied the strength that kept her proud through all the difficult years.

She had always been small of stature. Yet one would think her shoulders were those of a bodybuilder by the way she carried sorrow. Her life was not easy. Religion and pride kept her locked in a marriage where her husband's binge drinking was about all she could count on. She was the good sailor, keeping the boat of family afloat. At times she took refuge with her three boys in her sister's home, while the whiskey storms spent themselves, and her husband, curled like a mollusk on the day-bed, took a week to crawl back into sobriety.

During World War II, when her youngest child was four, she went to work on Wall Street. This was long before Wall Street was the behemoth engine of world finance it eventually became, long before the Woman's Movement in the second half of the century when women's ability to contribute to commerce gained some acknowledgement. Ahead of her time, she retained her maiden name. For twenty years, Monday through Friday, she got her boys off to school, in white button-down shirts she ironed the previous Saturday, before boarding the subway to take her from Brooklyn into New York City, where she worked as the credit manager for a sugar brokerage firm. At five o'clock she took the subway back to Brooklyn, where she filled the pressure cooker with chicken and potatoes and fed her boys within thirty minutes of arriving home.

I never heard her complain. Not even the day when, full of a mother's pride, she sat alone in a huge stadium as the first of her sons graduated from college. Her husband was too drunk to share the occasion. Not even that day when the United States Marine folded, then handed her the flag that had been draped over the casket of her oldest son. She stood erect between her two remaining boys and remembered to thank the marine as he saluted her.

A classy lady, even when she could no longer walk, she cared if her dress matched her shoes, if her slip hung, if her hair was disheveled, her nails ragged.

The morning of her death, I watched as the nursing home aide leaned over the bars of the bed and closed her eyes for the last time. I thought about the days ahead—the funeral and open casket, the "viewing," that tradition of Irish families. How it would hurt her pride to have the living observe what dying had left of her. I knew she would recoil at her own shriveled face, the tearful whispers at the casket, "What a shame, she always looked so good." How she would shrink from her grandchildren's exposure to the last good-bye. How she loved to be pretty.

After leaving the nursing facility that morning, I returned home and went directly to my bedroom closet. I rummaged in the back recesses, behind outfits I no longer wore but refused to part with, until I felt the plastic dry cleaning bag that held the fuchsia dress. I gathered the tiny pearl earrings, a gift from one of her granddaughters on a long-ago Christmas, and the framed photograph of her at her seventieth birthday party where she glowed with joy. I took them with me and drove to the funeral parlor to make final arrangements.

"This is how she looked when she was well," I said to the funeral director as I handed him the photograph and the few items. He nodded as if he understood what I could not acknowledge. He hung the dress on the back of his office door and placed the shopping bag with shoes, stockings, slip, earrings, rosary beads, and photograph on the floor next to it.

I dreaded the viewing, dreaded walking up to that coffin as I anticipated Nanny's humiliation. I felt I was letting her down, failing to protect her from an onslaught of pity that she never allowed in her orbit and that I was sure was imminent.

As I approached the casket the following evening, I kept my eyes averted, trained onto the sprays of flowers surrounding her body, forestalling the moment of betrayal. As I lowered myself onto the kneeler next to the coffin, I let my eyes find her face. Joy flooded me. She was beautiful! Her face had been re-sculptured by someone at the funeral parlor. This unacknowledged artist restored her face and gave the woman in the photograph back to us. Even her lipstick matched her fuchsia dress.

I felt giddy with happiness. Now she could truly rest in peace, her dignity restored for this last good-bye. In this moment of recognition I felt we shared a secret, a private joke between two women. How I would have loved to talk to her about it, like we had pulled something off, a great caper on the world.

The days of her wake and funeral were not painful. I greeted mourners and we talked about Nanny's life, her being ahead of the times when she worked as a sugar broker, her strength in keeping her family together, her love for her grandchildren and how great she looked in her fuchsia dress. Following the funeral, people came back to our house for food and winding down. After they'd all gone home the house seemed hushed, sapped of all the energy that goes into marking the rituals of dying.

In spite of being very tired that night, I was not able to sleep. I got out of bed around 2:00 a.m., made a cup of tea and picked up a magazine to flip through. Yet I could not sit still. I needed to do something, take action, any action to re-ignite life. I looked toward the darkened family room where the big bow window held the ivy, asparagus fern, ficus, philodendron, schefflera, and the wandering jew I had neglected in the previous days. It seemed as good a time as any to water them. I made my way into the kitchen for the watering can, filled it and returned to the window. As I bent to the task, I saw in the moonlight flooding the room a sudden flash of color touching the corner of the pane of glass. I put down the watering can and with both hands reached into the abundance of glossy green branching stems of the Christmas cactus Nanny had given me years before. The flat, broad, tooth-edged sections had grown to a huge size over time, sturdy, strong and beautiful in spite of never having bloomed.

I caught my breath. In the cactus's bed of shining winter leaves, pressed against the window as though reaching for the light, an infusion of blossoms fell like a waterfall over the rim of the glazed pot. They were fuchsia fuchsia fuchsia, and they were calling to me.

A sense of the transcendent caught me. And having read Thomas Merton's *Seven Story Mountain*, I had his vocabulary with which to explain the experience to myself: "It was as though I were accessing a knowledge that bypassed all my senses and struck directly at the heart of truth." My memory of the fuchsia dress merged with the fuchsia blossoms and ignited an intuition in me —*Nanny is here with me*. A wordless understanding flooded me and I felt a connection to that ineffable more, to things unseen but known.

Within a few days the plant was bare again, but that didn't matter. It had bloomed; it had spoken to me. When four months later, on Mother's Day, it suddenly bloomed again, I could only shake my head and laugh. My mother-in-law and I had another secret we were sharing.

I have often wondered if reading about Taylor Caldwell's resurrection lilies contributed to my being open to my mother-in-law's presence when the fuchsia Christmas cactus bloomed. I don't know. But what I do know is having read about Taylor Caldwell's experience, I became more comfortable sharing my own story. This in turn has led others to relinquish their inhibitions and share moments of inexplicable and consoling *presence* with me.

Chapter 13

The Yellow Balloon

I HAD NO WAY OF KNOWING in 1954, when Barbara sat down next to me and smiled that September morning in sophomore Latin, that fifty years later I would be attempting to tell her story.

Perhaps, all those years ago, it was our shared inability to master the declension of nouns in that ancient language that drew us together. Perhaps it was the fact that lunch followed Latin. I, being geographically challenged by the labyrinth of hallways in the school, was only too happy to attach myself to someone who could actually find the cafeteria as two thousand girls poured out of classrooms. Only in retrospect could I identify that shy smile between teenagers as the first hesitant thread of a friendship that would be woven into the tapestry of our lives.

In the years following graduation, we went our different ways, but the thread never broke. I went into an early marriage and Barbara into a career as an airline stewardess, at a time when flying was a coveted experience of travel and glamour. It was not surprising Barbara was chosen. She was not only bright, but a natural beauty, one of those women who turned heads yet remained innocent of the fact that she did so. I never saw her in her Pan American uniform but can only imagine how striking she must have been with her perfect features and ready smile.

Fifty years later we sat in a red vinyl booth across from each other, our salads untouched on the restaurant table. Barbara was mining the deepest part of herself for the ore in her experience with her son Douglas that best accounted for her transformation. Douglas was more present in his absence than the clusters of people coming and going in this busy restaurant throughout our three-hour lunch. I scribbled her exact words into my notebook. I had heard bits and pieces of her story over the years, but like ingredients for a recipe before they are blended, it had never come together, never really jelled. I wanted to get it right. I listened.

IT ALL STARTED on a perfectly ordinary morning in the late eighties. Barbara's house awakened as it did every morning to the mad dash for showers as Douglas, who was thirteen, and his sister Lisa, three years older, relinquished the last remnants of sleep to get up for school. It used to be three kids vying for the last shower but Paul Jr. was away at college. This translated to another five minutes of sleep for the others.

Douglas was at the kitchen table gulping down French toast and checking the Yankee box scores. His head was still wet from his morning shower, and Barbara had taken advantage of his pre-occupation with the scores to plug in the hair dryer and get at the dripping water.

"I know it was silly," she said to me, "but I thought he would catch a cold if he went out with a wet head." I knew what she meant. As a mother I identified with her effort to keep her child free from a cold even if the attempt was based on superstition.

That morning she knew she had to be quick. He'd notice her hovering in about thirty seconds and duck away. As she ruffled through the hair that covered his ears, her hand slipped. Here Barbara hesitated in the telling. Her voice faltered and she got a far-away look on her face, as if in that hesitation she could hit the pause button, rewind the scene, keep it from going forward. For, like all tragedy, there is that moment before the moment when life is forever altered. This was that moment. Her hand brushed Douglas's neck where, almost imperceptible, she felt a golf ball–sized lump. Her awareness froze; her heart plummeted. She turned off the hair dryer, "What's this on your neck, Doug? Let me see."

But he was already heading for the door, his ever-present smile disarming her. "Not now, Mom. I'm late for school. It's nothing."

All day the lump lodged in her mind like something underwater that she couldn't grasp. *Maybe I imagined it. Don't panic,* she told herself. *Wait a day or two. See if the lump subsides.* Looking around the kitchen, she saw the half empty box of antihistamine tablets she had been giving him for itchy eyes, the pink bottle of Pepto-Bismol for an occasional stomachache. His gym bag, cleats, the red-and-white freshman soccer uniform she threw in the washing machine every night was counterpoint to the medicines. She knew he was frequently tired, but he was going to soccer practice every day, so it was reasonable for him to be tired. Her thoughts rushed to his back-to-school physical two months earlier—perfect health, no problems. She had no sooner convinced herself that her boy was fine than her mind flitted back to the lump. She was scared.

The following day, the doctor's face wore a map of concern as he examined Douglas. He ordered tests. Within forty- eight hours they knew. Douglas had stage four Hodgkins disease.

For the next two years, instead of driving to the community college to teach literature, Barbara drove Doug to Hackensack Hospital for treatments. Doctors took the place of her students and faculty friends. Research on chemotherapy and survival rates of children with cancer replaced the novels she loved reading for the courses she taught. Each night she fell asleep clutching her rosary, remembering the advice of a nun who taught her in fifth grade: "Work as if everything depended upon you, pray as if everything depended upon God." She could do that.

And so she prayed for good days, good hours, and good minutes. She prayed for a cure. She prayed that Doug's hair would remain rooted, and when it fell out she prayed that the kids wouldn't tease him for being bald, and finally she prayed that his hair would grow back.

And it happened. Total remission. The nurses threw a party with balloons and pizza. Doug's doctors all came and toasted him with Snapple and baseball stories. Barbara and Paul took him to Sports Authority, where they bought new sneakers and soccer balls. That weekend Paul Jr. and Lisa, who had left for college the previous year, came home and high-fived their little brother. Barbara got out the good china, hung balloons from the dining room fixture, lit candles and cooked a family dinner of thanksgiving. She looked around the table at her husband and three children in gratitude. Douglas had withstood the fire of this illness, but each one of them had been scalded and diminished by its heat. Life was finally going to be normal.

As she unpacked groceries from the car one morning two weeks later, Douglas called from school. He had a sore throat. Barbara wasn't concerned as she drove up to school to pick him up. Lots of kids had a virus that was going around, and she knew it would just have to run its course. But as the other kids regained energy and returned to school, Douglas got worse. His team of doctors, the same doctors who toasted him weeks earlier, met them in the emergency room. A secondary infection had piggy-backed onto the virus.

Infusions of antibiotics were ordered. Within two days, Doug perked up. The crisis was over, and Barbara left him with his dad at the hospital and went home to shower. On her way back to the hospital, she picked up some Subway sandwiches. The three of them were watching the Yankee game on TV and eating lunch when Douglas casually pulled the sheet off his leg and said, "Mom, look at this." Douglas's leg was blue from knee to toe.

"It looked like he had a sock on," she told me, the disbelief still reflected on her face all these years later.

She called a nurse. Within seconds Barbara was aware of the steady blast of "Code Red—Pediatrics" being transmitted throughout the hospital. Personnel came rushing from every direction. In the confusion of the code, Barbara was ushered from Douglas's room into the hallway. Paul refused to leave and was still gripping his son's hand as Douglas was wheeled past her on the gurney. Another child's mother gathered Barbara into her arms and held her tightly. The "all the kids have it" virus had attacked Douglas's compromised immune system. He was going into shock. The code ended. The hallway returned to a hushed normal. But the battle was just beginning. Barbara and Paul made their way to the chapel to beg God for their son's life.

SIX HOURS LATER, she was done with God. It was over. Like robots, they went home and made calls to everyone who had rejoiced with them a few weeks earlier. I can still remember my own railing "No!" on the phone when I heard the words, "We lost Douglas last night."

FOR WEEKS, BARBARA had no desire to leave the house. At home, Douglas smiled at her from the altar she created in the kitchen out of fourteen years of photographs. His room was a magnet where posters of baseball icons hung on the walls and sneakers lay piled on the closet floor. His bed beckoned her. Lying between the sheets in the darkened room, she could almost find him in his scent, which still clung to the navy-blue comforter, the down pillow.

A few weeks after the funeral, Christmas holidays loomed. Seeking a geography devoid of memories of Doug, they decided to travel far away. They went to Hawaii. Still, Barbara's yearning for him was a physical pain always with her. It was as though she were pregnant again, carrying her dead son, not in her womb, but in her thighs.

When they returned home in January, she vowed to push herself to be herself. She owed it to Lisa and Paul Jr. She saw the worry on her husband's face. She joined Compassionate Friends, sought spiritual counseling, went to therapy. Still every minute, heavy as stone, crushed unremittingly. Fitful sleep served only to hurl her into her new reality upon awakening–she would never see her son again.

She tried to hide the depth of her grief from others. Yet six months later, Lisa and Paul Jr. found her crying in Douglas's room.

"You've to get out of the house, Mom," each of them urged.

Barbara knew they were right. She vowed to try harder. In April, she got a job as a design consultant at a furniture store. Each day as she drove to work she wrapped her blue glass rosary beads around her right hand as she grasped the wheel. Since Douglas's death, she was finished with God, but she identified with Mary, his mother, the patron of the rosary. Hadn't Mary watched her own son die on the cross? She would understand a mother's grief. The rosary beads connected her to Mary, a talisman she used to control her darkest desire.

At this point in her story, Barbara could not continue speaking. Her face reddened as shame overtook her.

"What?" I asked.

She hesitated, then whispered, "I didn't want to live without Douglas. I had this impulse to drive head-on into a tree, and I was terrified for myself and my family."

Yet at the furniture store, amidst the upholstered couches and gleaming displays of faux rooms, a feather of change alighted on the shoulders of her sorrow.

Providence or coincidence? All these years later, she still wonders.

She was only at the job three weeks when she was summoned to the design floor to assist a new customer looking for bookcases. Eventually they sat down at Barbara's desk and as she proceeded to open a glossy catalogue to supplement what was in the showroom, the woman blurted out, "I get a lot of peace from the rosary." The sentence was so out of context, it stunned Barbara. She doubted what she heard. "What did you say?"

The woman repeated, "I get a lot of peace from the rosary." Barbara heard the word *rosary* again. Like a disembodied hook, it snared her and reeled her in.

Barbara responded simply, "I could use some peace in my life."

"What happened to you?" the woman asked.

Barbara felt like a rock had been hurled through the wall of reserve and privacy she had erected around her public face. The mask of her professional self dissolved, and she told the woman about Douglas. It wasn't hard. In the retelling, he came alive again for her. Barbara told the woman about the joy on her boy's face when on his fourteenth birthday his name exploded in lights above the scoreboard at Yankee Stadium. She told of Douglas's excitement only fifteen months ago. The Make a Wish Foundation had arranged for the Giants' linesman, George Martin, to visit him at the hospital. She told of the day the drummer with Bruce Springsteen's E Street Band, Max Weinberg, came to the hospital. She told of Douglas's recovery from Hodgkins Disease.

But then the inevitable ending. Barbara could not prolong the story, could not change the ending.

The woman listened without interrupting until Barbara was quiet.

"Let me tell you about Medjugorje," the woman said.

"Medjugorje?" Barbara had never heard of the place.

"It's a place of miracles in Bosnia in Eastern Europe where thousands have regained peace through the rosary. It helped me regain peace."

The stranger woman went on to tell about apparitions of the Virgin Mary to six children in a mountain village in Bosnia in 1981. Barbara feigned attention, but the woman had already lost her with talk of miracles. A far as Barbara was concerned, there were no miracles, or, if there were, they were for other people: saints, mystics, martyrs, not an ordinary person like her. Hadn't she prayed for a miracle and gotten a dead son instead?

After the woman left, without buying anything, their conversation both lingered with and disturbed Barbara. An abstract image of peace through the rosary morphed into the literal image of the rosary beads she entwined in her hand each morning and evening in the car, her unprayed prayer, and the reminder to stay alive. *Could they be connected?* The thought no sooner surfaced than she discounted it. *More likely the woman intuited my sadness, or a misguided do-gooder sent her to the store to seek me out with talk of miracles.*

"I decided to forget the whole incident," Barbara told me.

But the following day, there she was again. Barbara saw her enter the reception area, an unlikely ambassador of miracles in her designer coat and coiffed hair. Barbara hid behind a bookcase as the woman approached the receptionist and deposited a brown paper bag containing video and audiotapes of Medjugorje, including a segment from the TV show *20/20*. Attached was a card with the woman's name and telephone number.

That night Barbara and Paul watched the tapes. Paul said very little, but she knew he was not impressed. His silence was an effort to remain neutral for her. Barbara didn't know what to make of the awesome testimonies of apparitions of the Virgin Mary and miraculous healings. She desperately wanted to believe in something, anything that would help her find peace, a different kind of peace than the only one she was able to imagine—that drive into a tree that would allow her to escape her own consciousness, which blazed with the absence of her son.

Barbara called the woman the following day and every day for the next three weeks to return the tapes. The phone just rang through. Barbara all but forgot her except when she saw the bulging brown paper bag stuffed in the back of her desk drawer, proof that the woman was real, not some hallucination she had conjured out of grief.

A month later she was back, asking for Barbara at the reception area.

"I've been trying to reach you to return the tapes," Barbara said.

"Oh, I've been away. I went back to Medjugorje. While I was there I left your name in a petition at the shrine."

Once again Barbara was taken aback. "Why? Why me?" she asked.

The woman shrugged but didn't answer.

"Are you some kind of angel?" Barbara asked, as once again their shared reliance on the rosary flitted into her mind only to be challenged by the thought that this woman with her talk of miracles was more quack than angel.

Yet Bosnia was now dangling in front of her like some magic kingdom. What if? Did Providence send this woman into her life? What if?

She couldn't remember what it was like to want something, desire anything. Not money, not travel, not the sun to shine nor the rain to stop, not wine, not drugs. She didn't even feel anger, like the anger that was consuming Paul. *I am the walking dead*, she thought.

With nothing to lose, she gambled on a miracle. Three months later, they boarded a flight to Medjugorje.

Sixteen hours later, a cheer swelled in the cabin of the plane as it screeched to a halt. The flight attendant announced they had reached their destination, Bosnia-Herzegovina. As she turned toward the window, Barbara felt the final jolt of rubber on the runway and the cold on her forehead where it touched the glass. Sheep were grazing on a distant hillside, and the tall grasses alongside the airstrip were bent from the whipping wind. She wondered if the pilgrims were cheering because they had survived a bumpy landing or because they were anticipating miracles. How she wished she could muster a cheer. How she wanted something to matter again. *What are we doing here?* she thought.

She looked at Paul, struggling to retrieve their luggage from the overhead compartment. No longer the guy with corny jokes or the ardent fan cheering at Yankee games, his eyes dulled by sadness reflected a weariness that never left him. Yet, here he was, traveling halfway around the world with her because a stranger had promised her peace at some mountain shrine in the middle of nowhere. He was in it for her.

Nothing was familiar in the mountain village, not the chickens in the dirt roadway or the rusty vans waiting to transport the pilgrims, not the huge wooden cross on a distant hill, not the hawkers in the street selling rosary beads, not the Czechoslovakian language. She tried to conjure Douglas, but she wasn't able to picture her thirteen-year-old alive son into her mind.

Over the next three days, she and Paul joined five thousand others who had traveled from all corners of the globe looking for their own miracles. They exhausted themselves participating in processions, visiting chapels, climbing Cross Mountain and praying for a sign of Douglas at the outdoor altar.

It didn't happen. Barbara didn't find Douglas. Peace did not find her. The most she could say was that an ember of hope was ignited in her as she witnessed others who seemed touched by a transcendence that didn't touch her. But that was all.

But then one ordinary morning within a month after returning from Bosnia, as Barbara got in the car to drive to work, something different happened. Her fingers rummaged around the console for her rosary, the routine she performed each day to keep her safe. But this morning as she threaded the rosary around her fingers, a warm and gentle presence enveloped her. She felt as though she was encased in a bubble that vanished the world and filled her with grace. A knowledge that took the form of words and called her by name saturated every part of her being. "Douglas is very happy, Barbara. Be calm. Be calm." It was not Douglas's voice. It was not her own voice. It was a woman's voice unlike any she had heard before.

It was hard for Barbara to estimate how long the experience lasted before it dissipated and ended. It seemed timeless but when she finally looked at her watch, no more than ten minutes had gone by. But in those minutes she was changed, the way a splash of blue ink alters the very structure of molecules when dropped in a beaker of water. She experienced a reality that defied physics and all natural law yet was more real than the ground she walked on, the trees growing alongside the road, the stone on Douglas's grave. It felt transcendent, something holy, a glimpse of the divine. It left her with the conviction that death was not the end. There was something more. Her boy was "happy, very happy." That was enough.

It was as though after falling through the ice of a frozen lake and banging her head over and over on the icy roof of her world, she had been suddenly drawn into air, into sky.

A sole desire erupted within her. She yearned for another such experience. She tried to recreate it, to manufacture it, to make it happen again.

But she couldn't. With the passing of days and weeks and months, the immediacy of the experience in the car was diluted. It became harder and harder to sustain the cascading joy it had provided. Yet the power lives on in her memory. It was a holy moment, her touchstone as she continued to struggle without her boy. It happened. Nothing could make it un-happen.

She told no one except Paul as her rational mind tried to make sense of the experience, infuse it with logic. She returned to thoughts of Medjugorje. Was this the miracle she had asked for? She didn't know and could never know, even as she clung to the experience as ferociously as she clung to the rosary.

Early in the morning, several months later, a rush of grief took Barbara back to the place she feared most. She could not feel the sun flooding the kitchen or taste the coffee turning cold in its mug. Doug's photo stared at her from the shelf. She was crying. Her mind screamed, "*God, I cannot do this anymore. You have to take me, too,*" as she asked the God who had abandoned her to do what she could not.

A voice answered her, and this time it was Doug's voice. It was in her head and it was all around her, a numinous presence. "You have to take care of yourself, Mom."

How many times had she heard this from Lisa, from Paul Junior? But this was Doug! He was there, a transcendent presence with her in the kitchen. He was in her head and he was all around her—as real as his baseball cap still hanging on a hook by the back door. Then as elusive as dust motes floating in bright light, the experience dissipated in the three dimensions of the kitchen. She tried to recreate it, conjure it, make it last. She couldn't. Yet, once again she'd been grasped, a knowing in the marrow of her bones filling her with joy.

Yet it shook her. *Am I psychotic? Hearing voices? Am I out of my mind?*

But the power of the experience trumped the doubt. Barbara hoarded it like gold. Her intuition told her if she talked about it, others might judge her, impose their own understanding on an experience that was meant for her alone. In the end, it didn't matter what anyone else thought. Douglas communicated with her. This was the core of her truth. Her son had broken through, which meant he existed in another realm. Death was not the end.

The scholar in her looked up the word transcendent: "that which is otherworldly or existing apart from and not subject to the limitations of the material universe." The definition matched her experience. She read further and learned that a transcendent experience can't be planned for or produced with intent. It was a spontaneous rising above oneself as if lifted by some higher power; an ascent of the heart, while the body remained connected to the world.

BARBARA KNEW THAT, for a second time, something extraordinary had broken through the frozen lake of her grief, and she had been graced. Her fantasy of crashing into a tree dissolved like a fog baked by the sun. It was no longer an option or a fear.

A year later, another instance. It was night. She and Paul were lost in a labyrinth of back roads in the mountains of Vermont. Barbara stared at the sky through the black windshield. There were no stars, only darkness, cold and forbidding, an abyss, emptiness, a nothing. She felt a renewed stab of grief. *Where are you, Douglas? Is there a heaven somewhere in the cold, black night?*

And out of the emptiness of that Vermont night, she once again heard Douglas's voice, "I'm right here with you, Mom." Happiness ruptured her grief. Time was suspended, and the lump of her sorrow dissipated. The unexplainable was happening again; the permeability of boundaries between this world of rocks and foliage and flesh had once again allowed the presence of her son to penetrate time. She remained very quiet in her seat next to Paul, trying to prolong the experience, but again, elusive as a sunfish underwater, it disappeared into the muddy bank of the night.

She said nothing to Paul as he maneuvered the maze of roads. She knew from her attempts to share the previous two experiences with him that it couldn't be passed on, couldn't be transferred. Paul had been happy for her insight or intuition or belief or knowledge or whatever she wanted to call it in Doug's continued existence. But second-hand explanations completely failed to convey the power or engage his heart.

On Father's Day, two years later, Lisa sent her father four Mylar balloons, each one a different bold primary color. The yellow one had a happy face printed on its surface. Lisa knew if an artist had tried to capture the essence of her brother Doug's personality, he would have focused on his ever-present smile. The not-so-hidden message of the yellow balloon was her way of including a shout-out to her dad from her brother.

Three or four days after the balloons were delivered, Barbara tied them to the back of a kitchen chair to keep them from floating around the house. The chair was situated next to the wall phone and soon the strings were entwined and knotted into the spiral telephone cord, making it difficult to use the phone. Barbara cut the strings and released the balloons, waiting for each balloon to lose air and shrivel up before she picked it off the floor and put it in the trash.

Eventually there was only one balloon left, the yellow happy face. It had floated across the kitchen ceiling and into the adjoining family room. During the next few days, Barbara and Paul glanced at it with amusement as it made its way into the foyer, still clinging to the ceiling before inching its way up the staircase and to the second floor hallway, where it settled for a few days like part of the decor that they hardly noticed. It continued to hover above them as the Fourth of July approached.

Barbara and Paul had avoided celebrating holidays with others for the four years since Douglas's death. The morning of the Fourth of July, they decided to drive to the beach. Here the vastness of the ocean, the hot sun, and the open sky erased distractions and helped Barbara access that dreamy place where memories of Douglas floated like clouds behind her eyes.

On the drive home, Barbara felt a renewed connection to Doug that made her smile. It was different from the other times. She didn't experience her dead son's presence or his voice but rather a link to him through memories.

"What are you smiling about?" Paul asked.

"Doug is with me," was all she answered, and Paul let her be.

When they arrived home, Barbara stopped in the kitchen to unpack the cooler, put the ice packs back in the freezer and drop the sandy towels in the laundry room. Paul went directly upstairs to shower. She had barely opened the lid of the cooler when she heard Paul calling her urgently. "Barbara, come quickly, come quickly."

She ran up the stairs, alarmed, not knowing what to expect. She found Paul standing in the doorway of Douglas's room.

"Look!" he said, as he pointed inside the room. She followed Paul's gaze and saw that the yellow balloon had somehow managed to float down the hallway, drop the three feet or so from the ceiling, avoid the entrances to the bathroom and three other bedrooms and maneuver its way through the doorway of Doug's room. It had descended from the ceiling and was perfectly centered in the middle of Douglas's pillow.

Neither spoke. They didn't have to as tears of joy welled in their eyes. Smiling, they stood in the doorway holding hands, and the strength of Paul's hand squeezing hers conveyed the unspoken truth between them. Douglas had reached his father.

Addendum

During the years following Doug's death, Barbara sought out grief groups to help her cope. She mentioned them in passing when we spoke, but I did not know any details of any group she attended, only that there she was able to speak freely, and felt understood by others who were also suffering.

In 2009, only days after Barbara and I met in the red vinyl booth as I prepared to write her story for this book, another coincidence happened.

I was invited by the librarians in an adjacent town to come to the library and discuss my newly published memoir. I accepted. After the discussion, a woman from the audience came up to me and told me she had been facilitating a grief group for over thirty years. She asked me to come to that group to discuss the part of my memoir that touched on loss.

I said, "Yes," and we made arrangements to talk by phone to discuss a date and the format. During the phone call, she told me a little bit about her group and its spiritual underpinnings. She felt parts of my memoir that were related to loss aligned with her group's mission and asked me to focus on those aspects of my book for the discussion.

As the phone conversation continued, we shared stories. I can't remember which of us brought up Medjugorje, but in a stunning moment of coincidence we both realized we were talking about Barbara. I learned Barbara had come to that very group all those years ago and told her story. The woman with whom I was speaking did not remember Barbara's name but she never forgot her story.

"Shall I ask Barbara to come with me?" I asked excitedly.

The answer was a resounding, "Yes."

When I got off the phone I immediately called my friend. Excitedly, I told her about my recent invitation to discuss my memoir with the grief group that was still active in 2009. And I asked her to come with me.

We went together. I sat in that room alongside my high school friend and listened to her speak to the group of about twenty people. I witnessed how love survives and how Barbara carries her dead child, like a light within her, every step of the way. Here in this circle of bereft strangers, I asked myself once again, is this coincidence or divine providence?

Chapter 14

Shattered Glass
1989

"Revelation can only be encountered by letting oneself be grasped by it, not by grasping it."   John F. Haught

MY FATHER'S WORKROOM was full of glass. It was stacked against the cinder block foundation of the basement between the furnace and his worktable. Rectangles and squares salvaged from old storm windows and plate-glass windows lined all the walls. Lugged home from demolition sites and neighborhood refuse, they were inventoried in his mind, ready to be selected for some future project.

His footprints still etched a trail in the sawdust that covered the basement floor. A neighbor's chair, its wobbly dowels glued and fastened between the clamps of a vise, looked like a modern sculpture defying gravity's impulse to topple. The radial arm saw was unplugged, a safety precaution he always took when leaving the workroom. Hanging on the wall behind the saw was the card "To Joe on your Retirement," signed by all his co-workers at the bank who chose to forego the usual gold watch that kept perfect time and gifted him instead with this shiny machine that made time fly. Lying next to the saw on the workbench were the plans for the birdhouse he made for me last Christmas and a carton of mechanical music boxes for his latest foray into woodworking, musical jewelry boxes.

I pictured him unplugging the thick black electrical cord to the saw, taking a soft rag and wiping the blade clean, a final check of the chair balanced in the vice before he pulled the cord on the single bulb illuminating the room. He had forty-eight hours left in his life, and he was on his way to the kitchen to make a ham sandwich.

HE WASN'T SUPPOSED to die. Certainly not on Valentine's day. A bad joke. A very bad joke. I was angry with him. It was funny the time he was hospitalized a few years earlier when he brought the big rubber dinosaur foot into the hospital and hid it under the sheet. I can still remember the aide doubled over with laughter at the side of his bed, the edge of the thin hospital blanket still clutched in her hand.

"He's gonna kill me with his tricks. I near to died at that ugly foot. Here comes the doctor. I'm gonna wait right here and see what happens."

But this was no one's idea of a joke. A pain in his side at dinner Sunday night. It persisted. The emergency room Monday morning.

"Nothing really wrong, but we'll keep him in the emergency room for observation." All day and still nothing wrong.

The resident said, "We'll keep him overnight, just to make sure he's stable. He can go home in the morning."

An hour later, "No beds. We're putting him on the pediatric floor. He can entertain the children."

"Go home," he said to my mother and sister. "I'll see you in the morning."

The call came at 5:00 a.m.

"What do you mean he's dead?"

Silence.

"He can't be dead. There was nothing wrong. He was with the children. He wasn't even in intensive care. Who was with him? It must be a mistake." But it wasn't a mistake. No one knew what happened to his heart that night, only that it broke, unreservedly, unerringly, while children slept or didn't sleep all around him.

Three months later, my sister and I were beginning the dreaded job of dismantling his workroom. Dreaded because the sheer number of screwdrivers and hammers and drills and wrenches and nails and paint cans lining the shelves in that room was overwhelming. Dreaded because this was where his spirit lived. His workroom was where he was most alive, plotting the next gift he would craft for one of us, rehearsing the next joke, the "gotcha" that would leave us laughing.

Where to start? What to give away? What to discard? The stacks of glass seemed the obvious place to begin. No one else would use it. No one else would be building glass-top tables, or painstakingly measuring an obscure corner of a grandchild's dorm room in order to craft the perfect bookcase or shelf to utilize that wasted space.

I would work on the glass, my sister on the tools. The pre-printed instructions for glass disposal as dictated by the town were tucked into the apron pocket of my rule-following mother. Each piece of glass was to be individually wrapped in doubled sheets of newspaper and the ends taped securely. Only then could they be stacked at the curb in piles no larger than two feet high.

And so we began.

Crawling under the workbench, I gingerly placed a hand on either end of the most accessible piece of glass, a two-foot square. I dragged it to the middle of the room and laid it down on over-lapping pieces of newspaper. Pulling each end of the newspaper taut, I folded it over, taped it, carried it up the stairs and laid it tenderly at the curb. Over and over I wrapped a panel of glass, ran it up the basement stairs and deposited it at the curb, all the while thinking about my father. As the hours passed, guilt that began as a fumbling of my unsteady hands settled like a dead weight in the pit of my stomach. I hesitated. I sat on the floor in the sawdust, my back leaning against a leg of his workbench. I asked myself, *Would he be upset if he were here watching me throw his glass away?*

The desire to hold onto my father merged with the objects I believed were special to him. I felt as though I were abandoning him. Did he know my struggle? Still another part of me could picture him in his red, paint-splattered flannel shirt, standing in the doorway, probably half blocking it as I tried to maneuver past him with some oversized piece of glass. He would have thought that funny, a cold Rheingold in his hand, as he teased, "Put the damn glass out—let's finish the job. What are you waiting for?"

He always had unique ways of getting my attention, some planned, some unplanned. When I was nine years old, I had to be at school at 6:00 a.m. for some project. The streetlights that illuminated Brooklyn were still on in the early morning dark, and my father got up early and walked with me through the empty streets. He walked the whole six city blocks with one foot on the curb of the sidewalk and the other in the street, like some lame duck, all the while repeating some nonsense word like "gippy-cackaruba" that he created to make me laugh. Actually, I walked in fear that I would meet up with a classmate or neighbor who would bear witness to this odd spectacle.

THAT DAY, IN HIS WORKROOM, each piece of glass foretold his intention by its shape. Some were earmarked for a foyer table that would nestle alongside a stairway, with a rectangle of glass flanked by two squares of glass on either side. Some were destined for end tables or medicine cabinets. Some would go into picture frames he constructed with coved molding. Slender pieces would serve as powder room shelves held up by brass brackets.

After a few hours' work, I came upon a random piece of glass buried in the pile. I caught my breath. Cut into a hexagon, it was unlike any other slab of glass in the room. I knew immediately a lot of work had gone into that shape. It seemed special. He had probably taken it to a glasscutter; all six sides were so perfectly angled.

I stopped working. "Do you know what he planned to do with this?" I asked my sister as I held up the hexagon for her to see.

"No" she answered as she took a break from sorting the tools. "But you know how he was, always helping people out," she said. "It could have been for anyone in the neighborhood."

We continued to search our memories for some clue to the unusual shape, but neither of us could connect it to any person or place. Finally I wrapped it and carried it to the curb. However, a sense of unease preoccupied me. It was as though I was a child again and had done *something wrong*. By the time I finished wrapping the last piece of glass, my unease had evolved into an overwhelming impulse to remove the hexagon from the rubbish. I needed it to be my "transitional object," the concrete symbol that would allow me to continue to hold onto my father even though I was turning his workroom into an empty tomb. The impulse sent me scurrying into the night to retrieve the piece of glass I had deemed "special."

"What are you doing?" my mother asked from the kitchen as I carted the hexagon back down the basement stairs. I told her.

She just shook her practical head. "That's silly," she said, "but if it makes you feel better, leave it in the basement."

Within a half hour, influenced by her no-nonsense attitude, I changed my mind and found my way to the curb once again with the hexagon. This went on three times—up the stairs, down the stairs, up the stairs, down the stairs with the same piece of glass. Finally rationality took over. I left it reluctantly at the curb, and, exhausted, drove home.

It was after 10:00 p.m. when I parked the car in my driveway and entered the house. Although I was physically spent from the day's work, emotionally I was charged with thoughts of my father. I needed to spin down, to get my mind focused on something else. I needed to cry. I didn't know what I needed. My husband went up to bed around 11:00 p.m., and I stayed up to divert myself with a movie.

Around one in the morning, I was startled by a loud crash from the second floor. Thinking that my husband had fallen, I dashed out of the den, through the living room, through the hallway, and up the stairs, all the while calling, "Are you okay? Are you okay?" There was no answer. I opened the bedroom door whereupon my sleeping husband turned over in bed and said, "What are you yelling about?"

"I thought you fell. I heard a loud crash."

"No, I'm fine, or at least I was until I heard you come bounding into the room. You were probably dreaming," he said groggily as he turned over and went back to sleep.

Shaken, I turned on lights all over the house. I knew what I had heard! I even went into the basement to see if something had fallen. Nothing was disturbed. Baffled, I returned to the den and resumed watching the movie. *Perhaps I was dreaming*, I thought.

It was close to 3:00 a.m. when I made my way upstairs for the night. Connected to the far side of the bedroom is another small room that serves as a dressing room/closet. I quietly made my way across the pitch-black bedroom and into the dressing room to retrieve my nightgown. I snapped on the wall switch. As the overhead fixture illuminated the room, I was stunned. There on the rug, in the middle of the room, was a shattered piece of glass.

I looked up. The glow from the three one-hundred-watt bulbs projecting from their sockets within the frame of the ceiling fixture was as nothing compared to the illumination filling me. I stared in awe at the shape of the fixture, now sans the glass covering—a perfect hexagon.

Time rolled back. Fifteen years earlier, changing the all-purpose laundry room next to my bedroom into a dressing room, I bought a new light fixture, one that would give me plenty of light. It had a plastic frame, stained to look like walnut, and in the shape of a hexagon.

Disappointed after the electrician installed it because the opaque glass inserted over the three bulbs greatly diminished the light, I called my father to solve the problem. He came. Using the opaque glass of the hexagon as a template he measured and cut a clear piece of glass for my fixture. He installed it. I still wasn't happy because the inner hardware of the fixture was exposed in all its ugliness, through the clear glass. Choosing beauty over utility, I decided to have my father re-install the original piece of opaque glass that came with the fixture.

All these years later, I had found tucked away in his basement workroom exactly what I'd asked him for. I heard myself laughing. I knew unbound joy as I felt my father's presence. "You certainly got my attention this time," I heard myself say as tears rolled down my cheeks.

"Who are you talking to now?" my husband, awakened for the second time, mumbled from the bed.

You wouldn't believe, I thought, but all I said was, "Everything's fine. Everything's just fine."

I would wait till morning to tell him how in the darkest hour of the night, a shattered piece of glass made me whole again.

Part VI

Synthesis

Chapter 15

The Many Faces of Consciousness & the Case for Post-Mortem Survival

"The distinction between past, present, and future is only an illusion."   Einstein

ONLY IN RETROSPECT, many years later, did I play the scientist, questioning what happened to my mind, my specific consciousness, in those moments when I felt my father's presence. A knowledge that was not intellectual, yet something known filled me and caused me not only to believe but to know my dead father was communicating with me.

One can only speculate what an MRI taken at that exact moment would have recorded. A current description of the brain alludes to eighty-five billion brain cells, each with ten thousand connections, a sort of wiring, it is speculated, when teased apart and mapped, will explain all of consciousness. Advances in physics and chemistry and neuroscience offer compelling evidence to substantiate the prevailing scientific view that the mind and body are one. That view would not allow for a communication initiated by my dead father.

In this mainstream biological view, consciousness has been reduced to chemistry and matter, specifically the matter of which the body is composed.

And so it follows that since one's mind and personality are products of bodily machinery, they will necessarily be extinguished, totally and finally, by death. The spiritual or immaterial part of a human being, that place where spirit resides—as Arthur Koestler has named it, "the ghost in the machine,"—has been subtracted in this view.

However, persistent in parts of the scientific community are those who point out that there are still areas of consciousness that remain unexplainable and scientifically unverifiable. Here the intuition of post-mortem survival finds a home, demonstratable but unexplainable.

At the turn of the twenty-first century, Edward F. Kelly was the lead author of a group of six neuroscientists associated with the University of Virginia who published their ten-year research effort in *Irreducible Mind.* Here they examined the previous one hundred years of research on mind and consciousness.

They cautioned that alongside the mainstream view exists another view that rails against reducing the mind to our currently understood neurophysiology. They illustrate how the discoveries of Newton, quantum physics, and relativity theory are forcing science to revisit the long-held beliefs that the reducibility of mind to matter is a forgone conclusion.

Those casting doubt on the mainstream view hold that the mind is not generated by the brain but rather focused, limited and constrained by it. The physicist Peter Russell directly refutes the mainstream biological view, stating in his book, *From Science to God: A Physicists Journey into the Mystery of Consciousness,* "Consciousness does not arise from some particular arrangement of nerve cells or processes going on between them or from any other physical features: it is always present."

In this view, the essence of a person is more than one hundred or two hundred pounds of flesh. A larger self exists with access to a cosmic consciousness that contains the past, the present, and the future—the whole of existence.

Without disavowing the current science and without claiming miracles, the authors of *Irreducible Mind* urge the scientific community to investigate those areas of consciousness previously ignored as too discordant with prevailing views to take seriously.

When considered as a whole, the vast accumulation of personal stories that touch on events that seem to defy natural law represent a body of experience too overwhelming to ignore. The authors point out a well-known scientific dictum: a right idea can never be definitely proven. The best science can achieve is to disprove wrong ideas. They revisit the complete body of scientific research on mind, including that which began prior to William James and persists in our current centers of learning. In this 800-page tome, I found a follow-up to those areas of consciousness, expanded on by breakthroughs in science, which William James investigated over one hundred years ago.

According to the authors of *Irreducible Mind*, among the areas of consciousness yet to be accounted for or disproved by the current science are extra-sensory perception and psychokinesis, which are often broken down into subtypes. The subtypes include telepathy, the direct or unmediated awareness of the mental state or activity of another person; clairvoyance, the direct or unmediated awareness of distant events or objects; and precognition/recognition, the awareness or knowledge of future and past events.

Deathbed visions are experiences in which dying people seem to see or converse with people not present, usually deceased persons, or perceive some environment not physically evident to bystanders. Occasionally, a bystander will also perceive what a dying person seems to be seeing.

Out-of-body experiences and near-death experiences and hallucinations are perceptions in the absence of apparent stimuli that have qualities of a real perception. They are experienced by healthy, sane people in a waking state as opposed to those determined to be pathological in origin or generated by dream or sleep states.

Veridical apparitions are cases in which the hallucination coincides closely in time with a death or some other crisis happening to the person seen or heard in the hallucination, even though the person experiencing the hallucination did not know about that death or crisis.

Collective apparitions are cases in which more than one person has seen the apparition.

The most compelling evidence for post-mortem survival comes from the hundreds of near-death experiences (NDE) that have been documented in different countries and cultures.

Near-death experiences are stories from people, often with no discernible brain waves present, reporting that while seriously ill or injured they left their bodies and were able to observe the surrounding scenes. They tell of emerging into another world where they met deceased friends or relatives before returning to their bodies. In attempting to describe their experience, references to overwhelming light, love, and peace are used to account for the reasons the person did not want to leave this alternate reality and come back into their bodies.

The increasingly popular interest in NDEs comes from the suggestion that mind or consciousness may persist and continue to function even after the death of the brain. Eight-two percent of people who have reported NDEs have become convinced of survival after death. The majority report a personal transformation that includes a relinquishing of a fear of dying and a sense of a higher power related to experiences of light and peace. These reports share elements of reports of mystical experiences.

A riveting story of a life-altering near-death experience is that of Dr. Eban Alexander as told in his book *Proof of Heaven*. A highly trained neurosurgeon, he had formerly rejected his patients' reports of near-death experiences as simple fantasies produced by brains under severe stress. His scientific training did not allow for any kind of consciousness outside the brain. When his own brain was attacked by a rare illness and shut down completely, he lay in a coma for seven days. Machines recorded the total lack of brain activity, and his doctors were on the verge of "pulling the plug." Yet he spontaneously recovered and lived to tell of his extraordinary journey beyond this world and into the deepest realms of super-physical existence. He writes of encountering the reality of a world of consciousness that exists completely free of the limitations of the physical brain. He emerged from the experience a changed man. Previously held beliefs about God and an afterlife were so reversed that he gave up his medical practice to devote himself to telling his personal story of an encounter with the Divine source of the universe itself. His work now lies in conveying his belief that God, a spiritual realm, and the soul are real, and death is not the end of personal existence but only a transition.

I am reminded of a story associated with St. Thomas Aquinas. Looked upon as one of the greatest theologians of all time, his writings from the eleventh century are still read today and form the underpinnings of much philosophy and theology.

Toward the end of his life and struck by illness, he was near death, but he survived. After his recovery, he told of a revelation he had while sick. It was so powerful and had such a profound effect on him that he ceased writing because he knew he could not translate his vision. "The end of my labors is come. All that I have written seems to me so much straw after the things that have been revealed to me," he wrote.

One can only wonder what this man could have experienced to change him so. Compared to the revelation on his deathbed, all that he had written was straw! His great works, *The Summa Theologica*, *Treatise on Law*, *On Faith and Reason*, *On Evil*–Straw?

Today, one thousand years later, we can speculate. Were Aquinas's words born of a near-death experience? These experiences have only come to be known and scientifically investigated in the last century with the advances in science and technology now at our disposal. Today there is a growing body of literature whereby people deemed clinically dead, without brain waves and/or a heartbeat, have recovered to tell their extraordinary stories.

In some cases dying persons have demonstrated a sudden revival in mental functioning just before death and seem to revive somewhat physically. These cases seem to indicate that in such diseases as Alzheimer's, the mind itself is not destroyed in lockstep with the brain. Rather, consciousness may be enhanced, not destroyed, when the constraints normally supplied by the brain are loosened.

This was brought home to me recently while listening to the oldest son of a friend as he delivered a eulogy at the Temple during a memorial service for his mother. Doris had been a poet, a wordsmith of enduring beauty. She had been eighty-two years old when a sudden deterioration in her health resulted in hospitalization and the use of a ventilator. Her son's words follow:

> This has all been so sudden. When my mom was on the ventilator for hours and hours, I was afraid I would never hear her voice again. But she was able to get off the ventilator sooner that anybody expected, and for almost two days, she spoke continuously.
>
> During this time, the tone of her voice, and her face, were full of expressions: of joy, surprise, humor, and sense of the absurd, as though she had undergone a transformation and was somehow able to shed the bonds of day-to -day existence.
>
> So as her body weakened, her spirit and mind became more alive, mixing memory, fantasy, and the present with soaring images and eloquent vocabulary. She had become what she had struggled so hard to craft and put down on paper. In my mind, she had become poetry . . . and she pulled me right in!
>
> With all the joy and expression she had when she read to us as young children, she spoke hour after hour and, yes, anybody would have called her confused. But to me, with her spirit fully out in the open, she was the mom I knew from so long ago, back again, speaking to me with the gift of her last poem.
>
> Memories, sights, sounds, smells were rushing in; gifts from our connection: childhood wonder, the excitement of being alive, the moment-to-moment anticipation of what will happen next.
>
> Perhaps during the almost two days of this soliloquy, inviting her loved ones to join in whenever they wanted, she had not only transcended the present, but was also allowing her fondest memories and visions to float back up into her consciousness, as a way of embracing all that she loved. As the end was coming closer, she was working to gather, distill and transform what was most important to her. Anyway, that's how I see it.

As I, and everyone else at the memorial service listened to this son deliver his mother's eulogy, his joy in the experience he was recounting was palpable. I can say the same for Dr. Alexandar when I heard him speaking about his near-death experience at a church in Greenwich, Connecticut, and for those people who told me the stories incorporated in these pages. Each felt changed by the experience.

Much has been written about "peak experiences," a term first coined by the psychologist Abraham Maslow to capture moments of intense happiness and well being, shot through with an awareness of an ultimate truth and the unity of all things. Peak experiences are not unlike mystical experiences described earlier in that they erupt suddenly, without plan or preparation, and put one in touch with a sense of the sacred, the holy.

Even now, when I look back on the decades I have walked this earth, the moment when the glass fell from the ceiling light and I felt my father's presence stands out, like a beacon, from the uncountable minutes that have gone into the decades of which my life is composed. That instant, when I so believed my father's energy had broken through a barrier that separates the living from the dead, was intensely spiritual. Some may argue the logic in it. I have questioned the logic. But for me, the experience was visceral and resonated at the deepest levels of my consciousness. It meant if my father continued to exist in some form, so did God. For that reason, the world and everything in it made sense. A sense of wholeness prevailed. A circle was completed.

Believing in God seems to be the personal fuel energizing my life and making a whole out of all that is disparate. I have often wondered what a peak experience is for others. As for myself, my experience in the recovery room after giving birth to John, as well as the shattered glass on the dressing room floor after my father's death, were among the peak experiences of my life. I continued to be drawn to stories of signs alluding to life after death. Amazingly, I learned they were more common than I suspected.

Chapter 16

Carl Jung on Survival of the Psyche

"We can not exclude the possibility that there is an existence outside time which runs parallel with existence inside time."

Carl Jung

ONE SUCH STORY that captivated my attention was that of the psychologist Carl Jung. During the eighties, while working toward my graduate degree in psychology, I became aware of his work on the collective unconscious, which he saw as the shared and inherited knowledge of the human race that is manifested in archetypes such as the great mother, God, the devil, the wise old woman, the trickster, the hero, and the shadow, to name a few. The collective unconscious has been described as a universal library of human knowledge containing the transcendent wisdom of the human race that mankind has access to and that guides us. A psychologist who distanced himself from the Freudian psychology of the time, Jung was interested in how a collective psyche was manifested throughout time and cultures.

In 1961, Jung wrote of a personal experience that speaks to the issue of the psyche surviving death of the body. In his essay "On Death and Immortality," he tells of lying in bed one night thinking about a friend whose funeral he had attended the previous day. He describes how he suddenly felt his friend's presence in the room with him and how he seemed to be asking Jung to follow him. Jung wrote, "It was not an apparition but an inner visual image." In his imagination, Jung followed his beckoning friend out of the house, into the garden, out to a road and finally into the friend's house and into the study. Unacquainted with the library room or its books, Jung continued to observe the visual image of his friend's presence. The image climbed onto a stool that stood below a shelf and showed Jung the second of five books with red bindings on the second shelf from the top. Then the vision broke off.

The next morning, baffled by the experience, Jung went to his friend's house and under the pretense of looking something up, asked the man's wife if he could go into the library. Upon entering the room he first saw the stool under the bookcase, just as it had appeared in the vision. He saw the five books, all with red bindings. He stepped up on the stool to read the titles. They were all translations of the novels of Emile Zola. The title of the second volume, the one pointed out in the vision, read, *The Legacy of the Dead.*

Jung acknowledged that the contents of the book did not seem relevant, but the title, in light of how he came upon it, was breathtakingly relevant.

In 1944, Jung had a near-fatal heart attack. His description of his experience while near death foreshadowed the many near-death experiences reported in subsequent medical literature, where scientific advances allowed the events to be measured and monitored. The following July, writing of the experience in his published *Letters*, he told of how it gave him a "glimpse behind the veil. . . . What happens after death is so unspeakably glorious that our imagination and our feelings do not suffice to form even an approximate conception of it. . . . The dissolution of our time-bound form in eternity brings no loss of meaning."

In a subsequent work, *The Soul and Death*, Jung writes about the psyche, the word created to name the seat of conscious and unconscious life. He acknowledges that no one knows what the psyche is and no one knows just how far it extends into nature. The continuity of the psychic process remains an open question.

Although it is not disputed that individual consciousness comes to an end with death, there is cause to suggest, as evidenced by the abundance of telepathic phenomenon, the psyche continues to exist after death, and under certain conditions can even break through the barrier of space and time. In Jung's words, "We can not exclude the possibility that there is an existence outside time which runs parallel with existence inside time." The foundation of this phenomenon is synchronicity.

Jung would later write in *Memories, Dreams and Reflections*, when considering such events, "If we assume that life continues 'there,' we cannot conceive of any other form of existence except a psychic one; for the life of the psyche requires no space and no time."

At the time Jung was writing, in the mid-1900s, the science of consciousness was in its infancy. In the last fifty years, hundreds of experiments in precognition, distant healing, prayer, near-death experiences, and other psychic phenomenon plus thousands of anecdotal stories suggest that consciousness is not a thing or substance constrained and limited to our bodies, but can operate beyond the brain and is indeed a non-local phenomenon.

The true stories that follow have contributed to my growing interest in pursuing the possibility that signs of the psyche continuing to exist after death are accessible to each one of us, through our own personal consciousness.

Part VII

Sychronicity

Chapter 17

Nana

A POET ONCE SAID, "Love can move mountains," but can love move a book, toss it from a shelf it has inhabited for fifteen years, and in so doing foretell the future? I'll let you be the judge.

"Beth is embarrassed." These are the words my son Dennis spoke to his father and me after his bride of two months, his soul mate, began to cry. It was Christmas Eve day and the four of us had been sitting in front of the fire, munching the Christmas cookies Beth had made in the kitchen of their tiny New York apartment. The phone rang. It was Beth's mother. Still carrying her mug of tea, Beth walked the phone into an adjacent room. Within minutes we heard her weeping.

The rest of us stopped talking, and I watched the color drain from my son's face as he went to her. Soon I heard the phone being replaced in the cradle, whispering between them, and then Beth's dash up the stairs.

Her grandmother, her dearest Nana, who had had a hip operation the previous week, was gravely ill. The operation restored her hip but a combination of trauma and anesthesia had destroyed her mind. Delusional, unable to make sense out of her surroundings, unable to recognize her family, the prognosis had gone from guarded to uncertain to poor. "We have to sell her house and put her in a nursing home," Beth's mother had sobbed into the phone. Robbed of a last good-bye, stolen by the quickness of her Nana's slide into dementia, Beth was bereft. Nana was alive, but the grandmother of gingersnaps and snow-white sheets in the guest room of her Pennsylvania farmhouse was gone. She was not going to recover.

We were all pretty subdued for the next few hours. At about 9:00 p.m., we decided to go ahead with our plans to attend midnight Mass and went about the task of getting dressed.

Dennis was the first to finish dressing and made his way into the family room. When I came down a few minutes later, I found him sitting next to the Christmas spruce in the tree-lit family room with a large book of Impressionist paintings spread open on his lap. I recognized it as an art catalogue purchased at a museum in France over fifteen years ago. He had spent a semester in Arles, France, while in college, and his father and I visited him during his break.

He startled as I entered the room. "Mom, the weirdest thing just happened," he said. "I was standing over by the window, watching the snow and thinking about Beth when suddenly I heard a thud by the bookcase. I walked over and found this book on the floor," he said as he pointed to the book of paintings.

I must have looked doubtful.

"The room was so still, I don't know how it could have fallen. Do you know what shelf it was on?"

I did. Normally I would have to guess at exactly where a book was stored but because of its sixteen-inch height, I knew this soft-covered art book did not fit between any of the bookcase shelves. For the past fifteen years it had lain flat, about two inches back from the edge of the top of the eight-foot-tall bookcase. Since it was only eleven inches wide and a quarter of an inch thick, at that height it could not be seen from any place in the room. Therefore, its presence did not destroy the symmetry of the otherwise bare walnut plane that comprised the top of the bookcases. I couldn't reach the top of the bookshelves or the book without a stepstool, and I couldn't remember the last time I climbed one to dust. No one but I knew the art book was stored up there along with glorious memories of actually visiting Europe and trekking around

France with my son. The book's slim spine remained invisible amidst the dust that settled on and around it, but I always knew it was there.

The laws of physics told me there was no way to account for its sudden movement and crash into the still room. Yet my logical son was convinced it had.

"*Oowie!*" I joked as I rolled my eyes. Dennis, my simpatico son, and I had often had fun around coincidences that surprised us both. Only in retrospect, well after the grieving, were we able to laugh about his spontaneous call from France all those years ago the morning his grandfather, my father, had shocked us all by his sudden death. His calls were a ritual of Sunday nights; never Tuesday morning. What made him call that Tuesday morning and ask, "Is everything all right?" He didn't know. So we had shared an *oowie*.

"I doubt it just fell, Dennis," I said laughingly. "It was lying flat on top of the bookcase."

"It did," he said, seriously. "The room was perfectly quiet and then—*crash*." And we shared another *oowie*.

"Maybe a truck went by and jarred the bookcases," I said, trying to be logical but knowing full well that there were no trucks in our residential neighborhood at 10:00 p.m. on a snowy Christmas Eve.

Now I was curious, too. I knew if the book had been hanging askance off the shelf, I would have seen it and straightened it. And in fifteen years, that had never happened. So with nothing else to do while waiting for Beth and Bob to finish dressing, my son and I sat alongside each other trying to account for the mystery of the hurled book.

There comes a time in life when, with delight, you realize your children have surpassed you in knowledge and ability. You wonder what more you have to offer. I was more than ready to regress and romp in a playground of times gone by with my son, the man who now seemed as curious about the thudding book as he had at ten years old about the mystery of his bunny giving birth.

"What page was it opened to when you picked it up?" I asked like the lead detective, a modern-day Sherlock Holmes.

"It wasn't opened," he said. "It was lying flat."

"Was it lying face up or face down?"

"I don't know," he laughed. "I just picked it up without really noticing," he said as he turned the book over on his lap so together we could examine the front and back covers. Interestingly, the exact same painting was printed on both sides of the book. It was of an eighteenth-century woman. She stood in the dead center of the canvas in front of a dark maroon settee. She was wearing a bluish-white slip and camisole and black high-heel shoes. A large fluffy white powder puff in her right hand suggested she was putting the finishing touches on her face. On the left side of the canvas an oval mirror on a wrought iron stand was tipped towards her. Unmistakingly, she was getting ready to go someplace. However, she was not looking into the mirror; her gaze was turned toward the viewer, as if she had been startled by something outside the two-dimensional canvas.

Dennis and I began to analyze the painting, trying to diffuse the mystery of the way it had imposed itself into Christmas Eve. Together, we created an interpretation in which desire flourished. We decided it must be about Beth's grandmother! We told each other that all the energy from the conversation that had taken place alongside the bookcase over the last few hours had converged and shaken this book and its message out of thin air. We agreed the woman in her old-fashioned clothes was a symbol of Beth's Nana, who was in her nineties. The clear-eyed outward gaze combined with her preparations to "go out" must mean that she was going to recover. Yes, we decided, she would be okay.

When Beth came into the room, I tried to lighten her dark mood by sharing the good news. She looked beyond dubious but was too polite to contradict this family that had succeeded in hiding their strange New-Age beliefs until now.

We left for Christmas Eve Mass and returned well after midnight. Dennis, ever the problem solver, was still preoccupied with the falling book. Evidently not satisfied with the story we had concocted, he retrieved the book from the top of the bookcase where I had replaced it. He examined it again. Each page contained an

Impressionist masterpiece and each facing page contained an abstract about the painting and the artist who created it. There were Renoirs and Degas and Monets and Manets. He studied each painting and read the accompanying abstract. Earlier in the evening we had not thought to identify the painting that appeared on the covers because there was no facing page and, therefore, no obvious information explaining it.

"It must be abstracted someplace," Dennis said, as he began to fan through the book while the other three of us busied ourselves with arranging the wrapped Christmas gifts under the tree.

And then my son all but shouted, "I don't believe it. Look at this." Inserted on the copyright page along with the publisher and author credits was the abstract he was looking for.

Cover
Edouard Manet (1832-1883)
NANA
1877, Oil on canvas

I gasped. Bob shook his head in disbelief. Even Beth took pause. Our hearts grew light. This was a sign. Nana really was going to be all right.

TWO WEEKS LATER, at Nana's funeral at her little church in Pennsylvania, my mind suddenly returned to Christmas Eve and our narrative of Nana's recovery. We had been so wrong.

When I got home I took the book from the shelf once again and looked at the cover. It was only then that I saw what none of us had taken notice of on Christmas Eve. Seated on the edge of the maroon couch behind the woman's back and painted half off the right side of the canvas was a man. His clothes were black and blended into the maroon settee, so the half of his body that was present was hardly noticeable as it disappeared off the edge of the painting. He was dressed formally, a top hat on his head, a walking stick in his right hand. He was staring at Nana and she could not see him waiting.

I sat on the couch in the family room, staring once again at Manet's painting of Nana. I thought about how I had so willingly projected a positive meaning of recovery onto its tumble to the floor. How mistaken that meaning turned out to be. Yet, this did not diminish the power of the experience. Rather, it folded my misinterpretation into the layers of experience that exists all around us. It reminded me how the wonder remains, regardless of the ability to interpret it.

Chapter 18

Signs and the Three Mothers

I T BEGAN WITH A TELEPHONE call from my daughter, which I had both anticipated and dreaded. Her three years of diagnostic tests and trials of various methods of conception culminated on this day, when she got the results of her second attempt at in-vitro fertilization.

Thirty years earlier, Kathy was diagnosed with diabetes a few days after her eighth birthday. For a child, diabetes is a balancing act on a high wire strung across each day and each night. Trial and error around the amount and kinds of food to eat combined with figuring out the number of units of insulin to inject four times a day were two instructors, and they weren't compassionate.

At the time of her diagnosis, it had been only seven months since I lost John and the existential questions about the meaning of life and death were still tormenting me. Although I could not pray for myself, I could pray for my eight-year-old daughter. If there were even a one-percent chance that prayer had spiritual power, I put my energy into taking that chance.

I prayed she wouldn't throw up on school mornings when she was forced to eat a balanced breakfast in order to offset the insulin she injected, or feel left out when she could not share in birthday cupcakes at school, or sustain running around in gym class without a precarious drop in her blood sugar that would cause her to weaken or faint, or get a good night's sleep without the interruption of a reaction, that no one would tease when she injected herself with insulin. And then I prayed she would be spared the litany of complications that may lie in wait, like blindness, kidney disease, and heart disease.

Since her diagnosis, I had been terrified about the dangers of an eventual pregnancy for her. While she was still a little girl I asked doctors how diabetes affected a woman's ability to conceive, to sustain a full-term pregnancy, to give birth safely, to have a healthy child. After being assured that all was possible, I continued to mine magazine articles and conversations with friends for evidence of successful pregnancies and births with women who had diabetes. Yet I was never able to put aside my concerns. They were visceral, causing my stomach to drop, my head to swim as "what ifs" permeated my thinking. What if pregnancy made Kathy's blood sugars uncontrollable? What if she lost a baby? What if she died in childbirth?

Now what she yearned for more than anything was the thing I feared. Yet whatever the risks, there was no choice for me but to support her. Love dictates. I forced myself to want what she wanted. My prayer was an odd prayer of rapprochement, as I both wanted pregnancy for her and resisted the wanting when all that could go wrong flooded me with intimations of loss. I wondered if she could be happy without children. Growing up as one of five siblings in our noisy, busy, chaotic household, she had more than once volunteered, "When I get married I want to have one quiet child." Yet the leap from one quiet child to childless was so much more than a mathematical equation. Prayer continued to be my antidote for feeling powerless, and now my prayer morphed into a kind of turning it over: "Let what is best happen."

I sometimes wonder if this seeking and reaching for God is encoded in the genes of the human race, the default setting when there is nothing else to do.

I look at the migration of tiny songbirds each winter. Weighing less than two tablespoons of sugar, heads no larger than quarters, flocks of tawny-and-white northern wheatears find their way from the Arctic to Africa and back again. A knowledge without knowing, a knowing without knowledge, theirs is a thrust for survival. I think of Emerson sitting in his study in New England writing, "The spiritual is not a realm apart from the natural but is instead revealed through the natural." A half century later, on another continent, Teilhard de Chardin added his voice to the chorus of praise, writing, "Man is drawn to 'The One' not by his reason alone; but by the full force of his whole being." Perhaps even when reason comes up short, it is the full force of one's being that suggests otherwise. So prayer became my bridge to resolution; the ground beneath my feet when all else was trembling.

DURING THE PREVIOUS three years of trying to conceive, my daughter welcomed my prayers. I knew she was praying, too, daring to believe through all the medical procedures that she was to become a mother.

The process of in vitro was as harrowing, delicate, and as time-sensitive as launching a rocket. I watched from afar as she gratefully endured weeks of daily hormone injections to control ovulation, followed by a "trigger shot" to control the hour of ovulation when the matured eggs were most amenable to conception. The surgical procedure to retrieve the matured eggs and fertilize them followed. Finally, there were the three crucial days of waiting. The eggs would either split and split again for the miracle of new life, or not. If they generated to a mere six or eight cells, the blueprint of a child of her own would be implanted into her waiting womb, already prepared by the hormones to receive it.

Elated as each step was accomplished, she called the lab at 6:00 a.m. on day one. All was going well. She called on day two. All was a go. Then day three, 6:00 a.m., the hour for the implantation arrived. Her phone rang. It was the doctor. Her eggs were no longer viable; the transfer was cancelled. The words pierced her with disbelief. Then a heart-rending sadness.

She heard the doctor's words, as if from some faraway place, "The cells are dying rather than multiplying."

"Can't you keep trying for one more day? Maybe they just need more time."

"I'm sorry. It doesn't work that way."

It was over before it began.

This was the first end. It was also the beginning of her second attempt. She had come so close.

Six months later, she would come even closer. The fertilized eggs were viable. The transfer was successful. All that remained was the two-week wait for nature to take its course as the cells divided and multiplied within her womb, followed by a test to confirm her pregnancy. Once again, failure. Her womb had sloughed off the tiny beginnings of the child she had already begun to love, the child not destined to be. She was not pregnant. She was shattered.

Motherhood was over before it started. There would be no nursery in the spare bedroom, no swing set in the back yard, no crayoned pictures hanging on the refrigerator door, no child in the Christmas photo. I could tell from her voice when I finally reached her later that day that she was spent from crying, spent from three years of ravishing her body with hormones, spent from hope obliterated. She was defeated and I was defeated with her.

Another six months passed. There was no more talk of pregnancy, but rather intimations of adoption entered her conversation. This did not surprise me. After all, she was the big sister of two adopted brothers. Over the years she helped them with algebra, taught them chords on the piano and extracted a promise from the youngest, Kurt, when they were both teenagers, to sing at her wedding. When her wedding date was set, he contacted the musical director who coached him as the lead in all the high school musicals. He rehearsed for weeks and sang to his sister. Adoption was another of the gifts that John bequeathed to our family.

One day over a cup of tea, she said, "I bought some books on adoption." I knew my daughter. Educating herself was always the first step of moving forward. Then in late September, quite unexpectedly, she drove the two hundred fifty miles from Washington, D.C., to New Jersey to tell me she was going to try in vitro fertilization again.

Anticipating more sorrow and wanting to protect her, I asked as gently as I could, "What makes you think it will work this time?"

She told me she had done some research. "I switched doctors and hospitals," she said as she gave me the statistics of live births with this new team of doctors.

I must have raised my eyebrows in doubt, yet I could tell she wanted me on board. Her eyes were asking for approval even if her words were not.

"And there's something else," she said. "Remember the last time, that day I learned I was not pregnant?"

"Yes," I said. I would never forget that call.

"Something really extraordinary happened that day that gave me hope. I haven't talked about it before, but I think you'll understand."

"What happened?"

"After I got the call that I wasn't pregnant, I tried to go on with my day at work, but I was a mess. I couldn't stop crying. I left the office and went home early. I cried the whole drive home. When I got to the house I just lay on the couch, for I don't know how long, crying. I didn't even answer the phone the first twenty times you called."

"Well, that wasn't nice," I joked, in an attempt to both acknowledge and hide my embarrassment at the need I had had to insert myself into her grief that day, to try to make it better, as if she were a three-year-old with a scraped knee.

She continued, "I eventually fell asleep. It was dark when I woke up, and I just started wandering around the house. I went into the sunroom where all the paperwork that I'd been too preoccupied to tackle over the previous months lay in piles on my desk."

She hesitated, took a deep breath and then went on. "Mom, you know all those plants I have scattered under the windows in the sun room?"

"Yes," I said, wondering where this was going.

"Do you remember the hibiscus plant you gave me a long time ago?"

I did. The plant grew from a cutting I had given to her a few years prior. I knew it would grow roots and thrive because I'd received my plant the same way, as a cutting from a friend whose hibiscus I admired when it blossomed every year in the big ceramic container in her living room. My cutting initially stood on my kitchen windowsill in a jelly-jar of water where tiny tendrils of roots grew into the water. When they were thick and tangled I transferred the cutting to a pot of soil. The potted plant thrived for more years than I could remember. Although it never flowered, it won a prominent place in my family room. As it grew to a huge size, the abundance of green leaves brought nature into the house even when snow covered the ground outside the window. After Kathy and her husband moved into a house with a sunroom, she asked for her own cutting. She repeated the process of growing the roots in water, planting it in its own pot and placing it in her sunroom with a variety of other plants.

"Did your plant ever flower?" she asked me.

"No, it still doesn't," I said laughing, confused.

"I didn't think so," she said as she continued. "Well, as I stepped into the sunroom that afternoon, the most amazing thing happened. As I walked toward my desk my eyes were drawn to a blur of color among the leaves at the corner window. I turned and walked toward the plants and saw it was the hibiscus plant you gave me. It was blossoming!

"Really?" I asked tentatively, still not knowing why she was telling me this.

"There were two perfect fuchsia flowers nestled among the leaves."

I still didn't understand. I waited and she went on.

"I was startled, confused," she said, "I thought, *why flowers today? On a plant I didn't even know was capable of blooming? Why two?* But it was the color, the bright fuchsia pink that flooded me with memories and at the same time gave me hope."

"What do you mean? What kind of memories?"

"Images of Nanny flashed into my mind," she said. "The story of the fuchsia cactus blossoming the night of her funeral bubbled up inside me. It was as though time just stopped. Mom, at that moment, Nanny was there with me. I actually felt her *presence* in the room with me."

My daughter went on to tell me of her overwhelming sense of well being in those moments, a sense that everything would be all right. She didn't know if it meant she would adopt a child or eventually conceive and give birth. Although she didn't understand it, she was momentarily filled with optimism.

I said nothing as I listened to my daughter. Not knowing what to make of this intimate story that obviously meant so much to her, I was reluctant to say anything that might dilute the joy she was experiencing in the telling.

Rightfully taking my silence for doubt, she said, "Mom, do you remember what happened when Nanny died?"

"Yes," I said cautiously. It was fifteen years earlier when my mother-in-law, a woman I loved and respected, had died. I remembered so much, but I had no idea what Kathy was referring to. "What do you mean?"

"The flowers, her dress?" she said.

Oh, yes, I remembered. The fuchsia flowers in the middle of the night, the image of Nanny's fuchsia dress, lit the wick of my memory. It only took a moment for it all to come blazing back, and as it did, a subtle chill started to make its way across the tiny hairs at the back of my neck.

"Oh, yes, of course I remember," I said.

As Kathy heard my sigh of recognition, she continued. "All of that came flooding back to me when I found the two hibiscus flowers blooming in the sunroom that awful day: Nanny's fuchsia dress, the cactus you found in the middle of the night, what you said it meant to you at that time." Her words came tumbling out. "I felt a kind of warmth go through me. I touched the flowers to make sure they were real. I slipped the stem of each one between my fingers and held the blossoms in the palm of my hand."

She paused to catch her breath, "Mom, I felt an excitement like I have never experienced before. *Nanny is trying to tell me something* went through me like an electrical current. Two fuchsia flowers suddenly blooming on a previously barren plant . . . I started to cry again. I wanted to believe it all meant something."

I didn't try to hide the tears streaming down my own cheeks. Hope stirred within me, as it must have stirred within my daughter that sorrowful day. With the lightness of a feather, something shifted. The event was ordinary but the experience extraordinary.

PUMPKINS CARVED into Jack-o'-lanterns grinned on front porches, and everyone else's children were plotting their Halloween costumes when Kathy's third attempt at in vitro commenced. Filled with foreboding and powerless to do anything else, I prayed.

There are probably as many benign ways of coping with anxiety as there are people who cope. It might be pacing or eating or running, to name a few. Mine was busy work. Without thought or plan, I would find myself in a closet or in the attic compelled to organize years' worth of clutter as I waited out a crisis. Always the mantra to the powers that be, the white noise in my head—"Let it be okay."

And so I found myself immersed in the contents of my night table drawer. There among the family Bible, Nanny's crucifix, broken rosary beads, brittle fronds of an Easter palm, and prayer cards for the dead that had accumulated over the years, I came upon a novena prayer card to St. Therese of the Little Flower. According to Catholic tradition, Therese Martin, the Little Flower, acknowledges prayer through a manifestation of roses. In her autobiography entitled *The Story of a Soul*, she wrote, "What matters in life is not great deeds, but great love . . . my mission to make God loved, will begin after my death, I will spend Heaven doing good on earth, I will let fall from Heaven . . . a Shower of Roses."

This was a nice story about a holy woman, an admirable woman, not unlike the narratives found in mythology, legend, folklore, and the sacred books of the world's great religions. Although literally questionable, the narrative of St. Therese was so appealing, almost magical in its promise to deliver a sign. It spoke to that part of me that sometimes chooses to believe, in the words of Teilhard de Chardin, "We are not humans with spiritual experiences but rather spiritual beings with human experiences."

I read the prayer and, obsessive in my knocking on spiritual doors, incorporated it into my daily litany.

I could think of nothing else but pregnancy during the two-week period of waiting. Yet my prayers remained ambivalent, having as much to do with my daughter being able to accept a future without a baby as with her having a successful pregnancy.

Let her handle the disappointment, let her conceive, let her handle the disappointment, let her conceive . . . was my prayer, the song of the fourteen days between the implantation of her eggs and her pregnancy test. It was the ringing before there was a bell for this "maybe baby" from whom I was keeping my distance.

Chapter 19

Roses

O N A MONDAY MORNING, late November, Kathy called and I heard her words bubbling as from some underground spring. "Mom, I'm pregnant."

I laughed, I cried. My heart quickened, and the world was shining as if the dull tarnish covering everything had suddenly been buffed to gold.

Bursting with news but unable to share it with the world at this early stage, I spent the rest of the day flitting like a bee in the pollen of anticipating, loving and thanking. Around eleven o'clock that evening I was getting ready for bed and realized I had not turned off my computer. I sat down at my desk and moved the mouse to exit and close the program, but instead I inadvertently opened an email. Suddenly my screen filled with roses. Someone had sent me electronic roses! I gasped and started laughing. I thought of the novena to St. Therese, the promised sign, ". . . I will let fall from heaven a shower of roses." What a perfect way to end the day.

Giddy with the intimations of mystery, I scrolled to the top and saw it was from Nancy, a friend and colleague. She had a great devotion to St. Therese and had once invited me to attend a one-woman dramatization of her life entitled *The Story of a Soul*. I can't say I found the play compelling. I was actually somewhat disappointed because it did not challenge my skepticism that existed alongside my desire to believe in miracles heralded by roses.

That had been years earlier. I was no longer working with Nancy and could not remember the last time I heard from her.

Yet, it was my memory of Nancy's belief in prayers answered through a petition to St. Therese combined with finding the novena card in my drawer that got this saint onto my radar. It wasn't the first time I tried to graft my faith onto another's, to believe what others found inscrutable. Yet I always fell short, always the "but" and a challenge whispering in the background.

During those months of Kathy's doctoring I think I would have prayed to the golden calf of the Old Testament, my desire for my daughter's happiness was so primitive.

This is so weird, I thought, *lovely and wonderfully weird!* I saved the email but kept its contents to myself, not wanting to dilute my high by sharing it and having my sanity questioned. My own little secret, a shower of roses not quite fallen from heaven, but the symbolism was close enough, the way they appeared on my screen bringing me joy nonetheless. I could choose to believe this was a sign. Or not. For those moments, buoyed by happiness, I chose to believe that all would go well with this pregnancy.

I called Kathy every day that week, needing to hear over and over that she was still pregnant, that it was not a cruel mistake or a psychological pregnancy brought about by desire. I was strangely happy to hear she had severe morning sickness, taking this as an affirmation of what seemed miraculous. Two weeks later, as we continued to revel in her pregnancy, I, only half seriously, told her about receiving the Internet roses in conjunction with my ongoing novena to St. Therese.

She listened very quietly and was silent even after I finished. Then she said, "Mom, this is so strange, there were roses all over my office on the Monday when the doctor called with the news."

"What do you mean?"

She told me how on that same Monday morning one of her co-workers had stopped by a vendor on the street who was selling roses. Although her routine was to dash past the flower stand every morning on her way to work, that morning, attracted by the unusual color of violet roses, she spontaneously bought a dozen.

"I actually stopped at her desk and admired them on my way in," Kathy told me. Before I could respond, she rushed on. "But that's not all," she said. "There was an event at lunchtime, but I was too excited and preoccupied to attend. It seems each table was decorated with a beautiful arrangement of roses. I know because one of my colleagues gathered up several of the centerpieces and brought them back to the office and distributed them on all the secretary's desks. The office was literally filled with roses on Monday."

My heart began to beat faster. I felt a smile make its way to the corners of my mouth. We were both quiet for several seconds. What was there to say?

Kathy had been showered with roses in what was either an extraordinary coincidence or an extraordinary sign. I didn't know. I just knew something shifted in me. Neither of us could trust the experience to words; like a perfect chord, we let it play itself out in our hearts as a sense of well being flooded us both.

I told no one else of this affair with roses; it was too fragile a happening to risk the raised eyebrows that might topple me from the "high" I found myself inhabiting. I only knew I felt changed as a result of the experience, more light-hearted, more trusting in the life of this child my daughter was carrying in her womb.

The weeks that followed were filled with joy for Kathy in spite of unrelenting nausea. She had her first appointment with a high-risk obstetrician as soon as the pregnancy was confirmed. Although she felt poorly, the doctor assured her all her symptoms were normal for the creation in process within her womb during those early weeks

By the end of January, as she completed her first trimester, she called and asked me to put her father on the extension because she wanted to tell us something together. When she was sure we were both on the line I heard her say, "I'm having twins."

"You're what?" I stammered. I was stunned. "How could it be?" I asked, mistakenly believing I had been aware of every detail of my daughter's pregnancy: every sonogram, every sneeze, every Saltine cracker.

"The doctor found two babies when he administered the first sonogram when I was barely a month pregnant. He told me there is often evidence of multiple births in the early stages of a pregnancy but it is not uncommon for a second or even third fetus to just disappear, get absorbed by the body."

We listened speechless as she continued. "I was afraid to talk about it. I thought it would be harder to deal with the disappointment if I told you or anyone and then something happened. But in my heart, Mom, I really believe I'm going to have twins. Do you know why?"

I truthfully said, "No, I don't know why you really believe you are going to have twins."

"It's Nanny." Kathy said. "It first hit me while I was still lying on the examining table and the doctor told me there were two babies. My mind flew back to that awful day when I learned I was not pregnant after the second in vitro attempt. There were two fuchsia flowers on the plant that day. That's what Nanny was trying to tell me. There were two flowers."

I had not given much thought to Kathy's belief in a message from her grandmother since she told me about her experience in the sunroom all those months ago. But now, twins? It was as if the dots were being connected, another whiff of synchronicity, another whiff of mystery.

I remembered the joy that had exploded in me the night I found the fuchsia flowers blooming in the moonlit window. A kind of grace washed through me, filling me with wonder. It was instantaneous. I didn't even gather thoughts and put them together to form a hypotheses: *Nanny gave me this plant years ago, it never bloomed, we buried her today, it is blooming, the blossoms are the color of her favorite dress, the one she wore to her seventieth birthday party, the one I saved for her wake, she looked so pretty in the casket, she is thanking me.* Rather, there was this immediate sense of *knowing.* It led me into unknowing, into mystery and an overwhelming joy.

Now with this incredible news, my joy doubled. The reality of being twice blessed filled me as it had my daughter. Already in love with Baby B, and at the same time fearing that he/she could suddenly vanish, my concern about Kathy sustaining the pregnancy to full term doubled with it.

During February and March, when the doctor anticipated Kathy's nausea would subside, it instead grew worse. The very scent of food, even opening the refrigerator door caused her to gag and heave. She was losing weight instead of gaining. Although her doctor was not alarmed, he was no longer calling her symptoms normal.

One of the obstetrical nurses tried to alleviate Kathy's worry and guilt about her inability to maintain a healthy diet or even eat. She explained that there is a parasitic relationship between a baby in the womb and the mother's body, and a fetus will take what it needs from what is already stored in the mother's body."

Old wives' tale or grounded in medical knowledge? I can't say. However, this explanation served to tamp down the day-to-day obsessing around the babies' lack of nutrition. It was oddly comforting to consider this magnificent feat of biology that was allowing Baby A and Baby B to find a way to circumvent the paucity of a diet that consisted of water, yogurt, Saltines, and an occasional egg. Yet to take that comfort, one had to block out that definition of parasitism taught in high school biology: a parasite obtains benefits from a host (the good news), which it usually injures (the bad news). Was a hidden fallout even then preparing to erupt in Kathy's body? I wondered. Each succeeding week of the pregnancy was entered into with the hope that this would be the week that marked the end of the nausea and vomiting and thanksgiving that although the symptoms were unrelenting, another week of development had passed.

In April, in the twenty-second week of a forty-week pregnancy, I got a call from her very early one morning. I knew from the flatness of her voice that something was wrong. She sounded disoriented. She had been up all night with excruciating head pain and constant vomiting related to the severity of the pain. Her husband had left on a business trip, and she was alone and frightened. The doctor would see her at noon. "Just pray, Mom. Pray to Nanny," she said.

Her father and I dropped everything and hastily made the drive from New Jersey to meet her at Georgetown Medical Center.

The obstetrician was concerned about a rise in Kathy's blood pressure, one of the symptoms of preeclampsia, a life-threatening condition as dangerous to the mother as it is to the baby or babies in her womb. The doctor sent her to the lab for a sonogram of the babies.

I sat on a chair next to her as the room filled with the swishing sounds emanating from Kathy's womb, the rhythmic pounding of the hidden world of the unfinished future. In awe, I peered at the screen as the technician moved the wand across my daughter's abdomen. The love I felt for the twins was exploding in my chest. They were less than two feet away from me but, oh, so out of reach. I wondered if through some alchemy of existence my love for them could penetrate into their watery nest.

As a lay person I was unable to evaluate the images on that pulsating screen. I alternately stared and squeezed my eyes shut, afraid of how I might interpret an image. Finally the technician spoke. Pointing to the fish-like torsos and large heads, she said, "There's Baby A stretched out as though on a beach, and squeezed alongside is Baby B, sucking a thumb and kicking like a gymnast." The babies were safe. For now, they were safe.

But the head pain was still undiagnosed. Was my daughter safe? Fear of preeclampsia rode the elevator with us, as Kathy and I went from specialist to specialist in search of a diagnosis. Finally, after myriad lab tests and examinations by an endocrinologist, a nephrologist, and a neurologist, preeclampsia was ruled out. Oh, joy!

Finally a diagnosis: a sinus condition brought on by the pregnancy was causing the blinding head pain and nonstop retching. Treatment was begun in his office. Within a few hours, the symptoms began to abate, and Kathy was sent home with a fistful of instructions on how to proceed in the coming days.

That night I slept in her guest room, my ear attuned to any stirring from her bedroom down the hall. I remembered back to when she was a little girl, and to those thirty-year-old nights of vigilance when insulin reactions during the night caused her blood sugar to drop to precarious lows. Low blood sugar could quickly morph into unconsciousness. One summer night, I had heard the unmistakable sound of the back door opening. More curious than alarmed, I followed the sound and went to investigate. I found my nine-year-old daughter in her nightgown, poised on top of the ladder attached to our aboveground swimming pool in the back yard. She had tried to find the kitchen to get orange juice, the antidote for plummeting blood sugar, and had instead walked out the back door to the swimming pool.

From that day on, I listened with a third ear, the way I imagine a whale or dolphin is attuned to their young, with some internal sonar inaccessible to human hearing. I would hear her stirring, get myself up, pour a glass of orange juice, sit on the edge of her bed while she drank it and then tuck her in as she rolled over to go back to sleep.

THE CRISIS SEEMED to be over. By the end of the week, Kathy was back at work. But the relative stability of her pregnancy was short lived.

Barely three weeks later, Friday, May 10, the twenty-sixth week of gestation, the delicate balance allowing her to function ended like a free fall from a trapeze. Desire, will, and determination no longer served her. Her body rejected and expelled not only Saltines and yogurt but also every teaspoon of water she tried to ingest. It does not take a medical degree to know that life cannot be sustained in this starvation mode. The doctor admitted her to Georgetown Outpatient Center for twenty-four-hour emergency treatment. It was Mother's Day. I insisted on coming to Washington. Even though Kathy assured me she was in good hands, I felt compelled to rush to her bedside as though I were the Red Cross and not a parent deluding herself about how her mere presence was some magical amulet.

As we drove the five hours of highway from New Jersey to Washington, D.C., I threw a never-ending litany of prayers at the God "of chance." Alongside my petitions was the acute awareness, backed by my own experience, that prayers are not always answered. Or the answer is "no." Or most devastating, there was no

God and prayer was an illusion. I had lived long enough to witness the unanswered prayers of a world where war was common and pain even more so. The "why?" of it is the existential question that remains unanswered. Is it fate, destiny, cosmic indifference, the incomprehensible will of God? Yet woven into the mystery is the amorphous suggestion that there is a reason for everything.

Over and over, we ask that same question. *Why?* Hadn't I asked it all those years ago when I lost my own infant son several hours after his birth. At the time, I didn't think I would survive, no less ever know joy again. Yet, that child who came and went like a comet in the night, who I never even held in my arms, left me with gifts I never dreamed of or planned. His was the gift of loss.

And so my ambivalent prayer for my daughter had been like a spiritual insurance policy. I was stacking the deck for a no-lose outcome. If the answer was "no," let there be meaning in that "no."

Somehow in the course of the preceding months, my ambivalent prayer, "Let her be able to handle whatever happens, and let there be meaning," changed dramatically. I saw those twins on the sonogram kicking in my daughter's womb. I had placed my palm on her belly and felt the tiny thump of a hand or a foot in my own palm. Now my prayer narrowed to the bare bone, raw petition of, "Let these babies survive. Don't let anything happen to these new and precious lives."

Kathy was hydrated, medicated, stabilized and discharged from the hospital, but within a few hours the symptoms returned. For a second time in as many days she was readmitted and the same protocol was followed. Again, the symptoms returned within hours and she was readmitted. This third time she was discharged with a medical pump that administered medication directly into her bloodstream. But to no avail. The doctor confessed he was stumped. "We'll figure it out," he said hopefully as he admitted her to the inpatient hospital for what turned out to be a ten-day stay.

Teams of specialists ran batteries of tests, and intravenous lines delivered nourishment directly into her bloodstream while medical interns swarmed around her bed with the specialists who were trying to make a diagnosis. After nine days of unknowing, the gastrointestinal team tentatively diagnosed acid reflux disease. Pressure the babies were putting on her internal organs in just the wrong way caused the problem. With news of this treatable condition, Kathy sent me home.

Although I reluctantly acquiesced, I left my heart and energy and prayers with her in the hospital room. She responded to treatment during the next four days and was finally scheduled to be released from the hospital on the following Sunday. I found myself preoccupied that whole day with a wordless mental prayer, *Let nothing more come up to prevent my daughter's release from the hospital.*

By the time Bob and I pulled into our driveway at home around 5:00 p.m., after a keep-busy afternoon, I was on edge, wondering if Kathy had called with an update. As we approached our back door, I noticed a tall, scruffy white pail standing on the steps. It hadn't been there when we left earlier in the afternoon. Getting closer, there seemed to be flowers peeking over its rim.

And there were! Wrapped in cellophane and standing in about eight inches of water was a bucket full of red roses. There was no card or note. My first thought was that one of my children had sent me a belated Mother's Day gift. My second, that the florist was unable to deliver them a week earlier when I was at Kathy's. *But loose roses in an old plastic bucket?* I thought. *No, not likely from a florist.*

Befuddled, Bob and I stood looking at each other. Suddenly a rare sense of wellbeing, an unexpected optimism enveloped me. It began to dispel the cloud of worry that had been following me around all day.

"You know what I'm thinking," I said with a newfound joy?

"No, I don't. What?" Bob asked as he fumbled with the key.

"Saint Therese, the novena prayer I have prayed every night of Kathy's pregnancy, roses, my worry all day . . ."

Bob, the positive thinker, who made a virtue out of not worrying until the evidence of a problem was staring him in the face, just shook his head and laughed incredulously. "Well, if it makes you happy."

And there is no explaining how happy those roses did make me. As I gathered the dripping stems to carry them into the house, I felt giddy with the gesture. It's quite a heady thing to feel your prayers are being answered, but the added phenomena of roses was something else. In that moment I felt as though I had glimpsed the Divine sense of humor, hitting me over the head: *Believe. Believe, you skeptic.*

As we walked through the door and into the kitchen, I saw the red light blinking on the answering machine. With the roses still clutched in my arms, I pushed the play button and heard, "Hi, Mom, thought you'd like to know, I'm home. I ate a scrambled egg, toast, and a peanut butter and jelly sandwich today, woo-hoo."

My girl was back! Once again, a moment shone with a numinous light.

By Monday morning, Bob came up with a plausible scenario regarding the roses, which he later confirmed. Five years earlier, as a favor to a friend's son, he invested in a small start-up company that supplied gas stations and local convenience stores with roses to sell "on the run." Every year, after Valentine's Day, a big day for roses, Bob got a financial statement from the struggling company, but never in five years had roses been spontaneously or deliberately left on our doorstep.

"While not exactly a repayment of the loan, the roses are probably a token of gratitude and not really extraordinary," he explained in his levelheaded way.

But I did not care about his practical explanation. I saw more than roses in that bucket. I saw another buoy in the stormy sea of my daughter's pregnancy, a sign that all would go well. And I was sticking with it.

My daughter's lounger and kicker each gained a few ounces during the following two weeks. The sonograms showed the combined weight of the twins was less than four pounds. Just an ounce's weight gain was cause for rejoicing. She had gotten to her twenty-eighth week! Getting through it was a major goal, when according to the prevailing statistics, a baby's chance of survival outside the womb increases greatly.

Two weeks later, feeling well, on Friday, May 31, Kathy went for her regularly scheduled doctor's appointment. Once again her life was thrown into uncertainty. Her blood pressure was alarmingly high. Preeclampsia was again the ghost lurking in the cells of her body. The doctor would see her first thing Monday morning, at which time he planned to hospitalize her and most likely perform a C Section. She was thirty weeks pregnant, ten weeks from her due date.

Monday morning, pacing and praying my way around our kitchen, I waited for Kathy's call. When it came, she was euphoric. Her blood pressure was no worse.

Now she asked if I could come to Washington and drive her to medical appointments during the week. I immediately cancelled my clients and arrived in Washington on Tuesday morning, June 4. I wanted to be there. I needed to be there. Perhaps every mother experiences this sort of magical thinking about her power to ward off the "bad" by keeping vigil at an offspring's bedside.

Assuming all went well at the doctor appointments, I could get home by 7:00 p.m. on Thursday, in time to see my evening clients. All did go well and by 1:00 p.m., with Kathy safely ensconced on her left side on the couch, I said good-bye and left to catch the 2:00 p.m. ACELA Express Train to New Jersey.

When I got to Union Station in D.C., I found it in chaos. A tree had fallen on the tracks in Baltimore early that morning and service was cancelled on the whole northeast corridor. When an announcement finally came over the public address system that a train would depart for New York at 3:45 p.m., I joined the mad scramble for re-ticketing.

When I arrived at the office, a few minutes late, my client was sitting in the waiting room, reading. I brought her into the office and, as each of us settled into our chairs, she reached into the large black leather tote bag she always carried with her. She withdrew a small glass vase and reached across the space between our chairs and handed it to me. In it were three pink tea roses, each stem individually wrapped in a saturated paper towel to keep it moist.

I gasped. She had never before brought me anything. In fact, she was a woman who was withholding in most aspects of her personality and this was a major change of behavior for her.

"You brought me roses?" My eyes stayed riveted to the flowers as I reached across the therapy space to accept them. A spontaneous wash of tears trickled down my cheeks.

"They're from my garden," she said, looking askance at my tears. "It seems like you've had a bad week, I just wanted to bring you something."

"You couldn't possibly know what these roses mean to me," I sputtered, as once again a moment was limned in light.

She cocked her head and looked at me quizzically.

The room grew quiet as we both dealt with the awkwardness of the moment. The mascara running down my face attested to just how undone I had become by her gift of roses. I felt I owed her an explanation and, unprofessional as it was, for this was the therapy space, honored and preserved for the clients' story, I told her of my prayers to St. Therese and all that had transpired around roses and my daughter's pregnancy up until and including that magic moment.

She smiled as our roles reversed. She listened as I revealed that most intimate and vulnerable aspect of my life—a faith that had been ascending and descending on the whim of roses. I feared she might think me daft, but the desire to share overwhelmed all my training to refrain from introducing personal information. When I finished, all she said was, "Wow," as she allowed herself to be drawn into the events in which she was now playing a part.

Kathy continued on the blessed bed rest for another two weeks. She laughingly tolerated me as I counted off the weeks and half weeks of her pregnancy. "You can't get me further along no matter how you do the math, Mom," she would insist during our daily telephone talks as I manipulated the gestational calendar.

Then, in her thirty-third week, she called after the sonogram. There was a lack of activity with Baby B. I froze. I couldn't even ask a follow-up question, and immediately translated "lack of activity" to "there *is* a heartbeat." Three hours later, a repeat sonogram produced the same result: Baby B was not moving.

"I can't talk. I'm being admitted. They are going to take the babies."

The phone went dead. All I was aware of was love, an abstraction that weighs nothing, but felt as heavy as a chunk of marble inside my chest. It splintered into a million slivers and flew to her. All I could do was love the three of them.

Preeclampsia was on the radar again. The day dragged into evening and evening to night as decisions to take the babies wavered with every hiccup from the monitors recording vital statistics on the three of them. Around 11:00 p.m., a change. Baby B was more than a heartbeat. Baby B was responding! Alleluia.

I ARRIVED AT THE HOSPITAL around noon the following day. Entering the hospital room, I noticed how prominent the freckles across the bridge of Kathy's nose looked on her pale face. She smiled weakly as I threaded my way between the machines and equipment at her bedside to give her a hug.

The timing for the C-section was a moving target, changing hourly with test results. Wednesday and Thursday were days of uncertainty and waiting as the monitoring machines ruled like dictators. Yet each passing hour was a gift of time to Baby A and Baby B as they continued to develop minute by minute inside Kathy's womb. The doctor had told her, "Every additional hour we can keep the babies inside you gives them a better chance." The magnificence of cells racing to put the crucial finishing touches on a lung, a heart, a brain, a finger was an omnipresent awareness as we waited. That moment arrived early Friday morning. The nephrologist had gone into the lab himself to examine her blood cells under a microscope. The preeclampsia was advancing. They needed to take the babies. A Cesarean section was scheduled. It was two days into the thirty-fifth week of her pregnancy.

Bob and I sat in a waiting area a short distance from the operating room. All was quiet for about twenty minutes, when suddenly one of the residents attending the C-section ran from the operating room and shouted an order to the nursing station. "Call the pharmacy stat and get . . ." Get what? I couldn't make out what he said.

What did they need in this vast medical complex that they didn't have? We could hear the nurse calling the pharmacy over and over, making the same request every few minutes as the requisition failed to appear. It was terrifying to imagine what was needed so urgently. The resident came out a second time about twenty minutes later and made the same request. "Stat," he emphasized. Immobilized by fear, I approached the nursing station and asked what was needed in the operating room. The nurse would not say, waved me away . . . but I overheard a few words of her telephone conversation . . . something about a blood transfusion that was waiting on the requisition. (Later I would learn that a blood transfusion was done during the C-Section. A second one would be done two days later.) After another forty minutes, the anesthesiologist dashed past us, pulling his surgical cap off as he ran. I was sure he was avoiding us. Forty minutes later, Kathy's weary obstetrician, still in his scrubs, approached. Why was he walking so slowly?

"What happened?" I ran to meet him.

His smile spoke first. "The babies were born. Baby A is a boy and Baby B is a girl. Congratulations; everyone is fine. Your daughter is in the recovery room and the babies are in the NICU" (Neonatal Intensive Care Unit).

"Everyone is fine?" I parroted, as if I were preserving the words in amber so they could never be taken back. "Everyone is fine."

"They are five weeks early and very tiny," he continued. "They'll have to stay in the hospital for a few weeks, but they should do well. The pediatrician is with them now. You can go down to recovery and see your daughter."

We rushed down the hospital corridor and opened the door to the recovery room. Her husband was with her. "Did you see the babies?" she asked from a twilight state of medication and pain.

"Not yet. We came to see you first."

"I haven't seen them," she said with urgency. "Go to the nursery. Make sure they're there. Come back and tell me how they are." She knew I could not keep anything from her, that my face if not my words would reveal the truth, as I knew it. Perhaps this was the one time she really did need me to confirm that nothing was being kept from her, that her babies were living in this world.

After scrubbing our hands and arms for a full three minutes with hot water and disinfectant soap and donning disposable gowns, caps, and masks, a nurse led Bob and me through the labyrinth that was the NICU.

The babies lay next to each other. Baby A, the boy lounger, was asleep. Baby B, his sister, was flailing like a little swimmer, as if to escape the flannel blanket in which she was swaddled. Their heads, smaller than tennis balls, were covered by knit caps. Baby A wore a mint green cap, and Baby B, a cap of deep pink, almost fuchsia.

The nurse indicated that we could touch them, but neither of us dared. The fact that they belonged inside the womb for another five weeks was dizzying. Tears unleashed from some well of wonder deep within me. As I stood alongside the little shoebox beds of these living breathing beings, there were no words for the unnamable reality that was present for me.

The difficulty of my daughter's four-year journey fell away like a carapace. What remained was the afterglow of signs that had so infused my faith during the previous months. There was Nanny in her fuchsia dress and the way I felt her presence the night we buried her. The hibiscus blossoming in winter. St. Therese and the promise of roses fulfilled with an electronic bouquet delivered to my computer. The violet roses and centerpieces carried into Kathy's office the day her pregnancy was confirmed. That pail full of roses delivered to my back door, and a vase with three delicate tea roses carried to my office. I was standing on the frontier of mystery, where love and prayer and desire combined in ways I could never know to produce this transcending moment.

Here, in the glass and stainless steel warren of the hospital nursery, the invisible nature of life poured into me. It filled me. It lifted me in a shinning epiphany of thanksgiving.

Later that night, as I continued to bask in the reality of these two new beings hiccupping and kicking in the nursery, I thought of the constant prayers rolling through my mind and uttered with every cell of my body during the previous year. I had, as William James suggested, relied on the keynote of chance. I had never ceased praying.

How else could I put it? My prayers had been gloriously answered!

Part VIII

Consciousness: The Link between Science & Religion

Chapter 20

Consciousness
Two Views

"When science sees consciousness to be a fundamental quality of reality and religion takes God to be the light of consciousness shining within us all, the two worldviews will converge."

Peter Russell

WONDER AND SKEPTICISM were my two companions during those days when the hibiscus blossomed and the glass from the ceiling fixture shattered and roses seemed to manifest at significant moments. Each instance caught me in a kind of glow. They were bonus moments bestowed out of the goodness of the universe. Although I could not understand how they developed or came to me, I guarded them and held them close—a secret stash of joy. They felt spiritual. Each one produced a wondrous *thank you* in my heart for the lightning flash of happiness that coursed through me.

During those years, I began to gather stories from other people with life-altering experiences that also seemed to emanate from outside time. I continued to follow theologians who embraced the work of Teilhard. As a result, my interest in science increased. I slowly found my way through these writings to some of the underlying science blossoming in the latter half of the twentieth century that this new breed of theologians were incorporating into their thinking.

A new story began to emerge, one as startling as Galileo's discovery that the earth was not the center of the universe and as unexpected as Einstein's equations that revealed the universe was not a finite sphere, but was continually expanding in all directions.

The greatest leaps in knowledge in recent years have occurred in the discoveries of quantum mechanics, where the focus is on the infinitely small components of matter at the subatomic level. Here at the molecular level, everything is in motion. Every atom is spinning around its nucleus, and all of matter, even what looks to be solid—the table, the mountain, you, and me—are ninety-nine percent emptiness with solar systems of atoms spinning away. It is because of the rapidity of the subatomic particles spinning around their nucleus that allows us to experience ourselves, and the world, as solid.

In the quantum world, the laws of nature that govern the universe, as we know it, cease to exist. Gravity, magnetism, time, cause and effect no longer operate according to the laws of physics upon which we rely. In their stead are the quantum laws of particles and waves too indiscriminate for anything but the tools of science and mathematical equations to approach.

Objects in the subatomic realm follow different rules. We can never be sure where they are or what they are doing. We cannot even say *what* they are because that depends on how we observe them.

In 1916, Einstein's general theory of relativity ushered in the field of quantum science, which led to breakthroughs in scientific discoveries. One such discovery established the very underpinnings of our universe as a heaving sea of vibrating energy, commonly referred to as the quantum vacuum or the Zero Point Field.

We now know there is no such thing as empty space. Matter of all types, that which is known and unknown, both luminous and dark, accounts for just 27.5 percent of all that exists. The rest of creation, 72.5 percent, is the mysterious dark *energy* inhabiting the quantum vacuum, that heaving sea of vibrating energy about which we know so little.

The cosmologist Brian Swimme, who is at the forefront of a movement to integrate science and religion, writing in *The Hidden Heart of the Cosmos*, offers us a way to conceptualize this vacuum. He asks us to cup our empty hands together and imagine what we are holding. Helping us along, he tells us that in quantum terms there would be more than a billion trillion molecules of air, such as oxygen, nitrogen, and carbon dioxide. There would also be invisible particles of light, like photons. He then asks us to imagine subtracting all the subatomic particles, molecules, and photons from our cupped hands. What would remain is the "vacuum," or "empty space."

He goes on to explain an amazing discovery. When quantum physicists investigate this vacuum, they find the strange appearance of elementary particles emerging or foaming into existence out of the nothingness of the vacuum. He asks us to consider a universe where the vacuum is actually an energy field out of which all matter is formed and from which arise even our personal thoughts, feelings, and instincts.

We now know all living beings are made of the same material as the quantum vacuum. On our most fundamental level, living beings are composed of packets of quantum energy or light that continually exchange information with this inexhaustible energy sea. As a result, we not only live in the universe, the universe lives within us. We literally resonate with our world and with each other at the undercoat of our being. I cannot help but wonder at the smile on William James's face if he were alive to hear of these scientific breakthroughs. I think of his words, published in 1902, ". . . the conscious person is continuous with a wider self . . . into which minds can plunge as into a mother-sea or reservoir."

Expressing this in scientific terms, Danah Zohar writes, "The quantum world view transcends the dichotomy between mind and matter, or between inner and outer, by showing us the basic building blocks of mind (bosons) and the basic building blocks of matter (fermions) arise out of a common quantum substrate (the vacuum) and are engaged in a mutually creative dialogue . . ."

Scientific work on holograms revealed that nothing exists as a whole. Everything is part of something else. Thus the web of connections underlying our interpersonal world is mirrored in the natural world of waves and particles, which extend into consciousness and everything that consciousness touches.

From a spiritual perspective, it seems to matter that all matter in the universe is interconnected by waves, spread out through time and space and carrying on to infinity, tying one part of the universe to every other part.

Who among us does not already know this at some rudimentary level? Not from the science, but from personal experience. Who can witness images of an earthquake in Peru or a tsunami in Thailand or a war in Afghanistan without resonating with victims in the depth of our being? Society holds its breath waiting for the rescue of men trapped in a mine or for the release of a kidnapped child as our collective consciousness rises in that direction, reaches out. And when that child or victim happens to be our child or our brother, we do more than resonate. Our physical bodies are inflicted with pain.

Each day, each minute, someone we never met or even imagined is influencing my life and yours for better or worse. It may be the doctor whose unique education allowed him to properly diagnose your sister. Or the teenage clerk in Home Depot who goes that extra step to find the replacement part for your lawn mower, saving you hundreds of dollars on a new purchase and prompting you to donate half of that savings to a food bank that will deliver food to earthquake victims in Haiti. It may be the mother of the child who is being born on the other side of the world who you will grow to love when someone in your family adopts her. Perhaps the engineer in Michigan, who will fail to inspect the car you will purchase ten months from now, setting you up for an accident. Or the author who will write that one sentence you have been seeking that resonates with your soul.

Aligned with the new story in science, theologians tell us no one religion can conquer the world as the sole religion. In this they echo Teilhard, who wrote of "an eventual convergence of religions . . . the convergence of psychic, spiritual energy, the unification of the whole."

Absorbing this truth unmoored me from what had become an untenable concept that had its origins in childhood—the idea that one religion held all the answers. I was transported back to when I was ten years old. My best friend's name was Beverly Nevins, and she was Jewish. I didn't know what Jewish meant at the time, except that in some way she and I were different. An undercurrent ran through our playing with dolls and selling lemonade at our little homemade stand. An amorphous something separated us at a deep level.

I recognize this now as part of the history of the world, a *my god is better that your god* attitude that continues to be acted out. We witness it in subtle and obvious ways as synagogues are defaced and children with suicide bombs strapped to their bodies are sacrificed in the name of religion.

WHEN I CAME ACROSS Einstein's early comment about quantum mechanics as "spooky action at a distance," I was further drawn to investigate what parallels might exist connecting the spiritual and natural worlds. At the time of his comment, Einstein could not believe what the research seemed to be revealing.

Not until 1982 was the scientific community finally able to offer proof of "spooky action at a distance" as the evolved tools of science validated the entanglement theory, known as non-locality. Experiments confirmed that in the subatomic world, electrons move from point A to point B without passing through any intermediate points, thus transporting themselves over space and time in an eerie omnipresence. What this meant was an electron could influence other quantum particles instantaneously, over any distance, despite there being no exchange of force or energy. (This phenomenon made its way into language as a cliché, as breakthroughs in thought or experience are often described as "quantum leaps.")

If something is non-local, it is not localized to specific points in space, such as the brain, or to a specific point in time, such as the present. Non-local events are unmediated in that they require no energetic signal to "carry" them; they are unmitigated, meaning they do not become weaker with increasing distance; they are omnipresent, everywhere at once, infinite in time, present at all moments—past, present, and future. They are eternal.

What this discovery meant, according to researcher Lynne Mc Taggert, writing in *The Field: The Quest for the Secret Force of the Universe* is that "at a certain level things could travel faster than the speed of light," a discovery that shattered one of the previously held sacred tenets of science. It further demonstrated the world at its most basic exists as a complex web of interdependent relationships—forever indivisible.

Many prominent scientists continue to refute this view of non-local consciousness. They hold that consciousness is identical to the brain, which would limit and confine it to one localized specific point in space (the organ we call the brain), and to one specific point in time (the present). However, as others speculate, if consciousness is indeed identical to the brain, how can we account for premonitions, extra-sensory perception, near-death experiences, and all those other forms of consciousness that hundreds of experiments and millions of testimonials affirm?

Some speculate that it is this sea of consciousness, suggested by William James, into which "minds can plunge as into a mother-sea or reservoir," that past and present and future exist as one.

These quantum laws override the laws of a Newtonian world that have shaped our thinking, where everything moves seamlessly through time. These laws are still not fully understood by the scientist, yet their existence has led many people to associate the paradoxes of the quantum world with the mysteries of religion and see them as a bridge to linking the material world with the spiritual. After one hundred years of delving into quantum questions, even the most prominent scientists admit to not understanding what they witness in their experiments and in the mathematical equations. Quantum events happen, but no one knows why.

In the scientific community, some believe the dogmatically held mainstream view that the brain generates consciousness or is identical with it will eventually topple. They believe the story will change, a paradigm shift will occur, and a non-local picture of the mind will emerge, affirming that consciousness is fundamental, omnipresent, and eternal.

This trend is reflected in the number of medical schools that have integrated courses devoted to exploring the role of the mind as well as religious practice and prayer in overall health and healing.

Quantum discoveries have led Mc Taggert to suggest "a life force that flows through the universe," what psychologists have called collective consciousness and theologians have termed the Holy Spirit. Now science seems to be offering evidence for what, over the centuries, human beings have had faith in but had no way to support. In essence, the new physics may be offering a science of religion as it confronts a life force connected to and touching everything, a life force transcending life and death.

Words such as these have released me from the need to tease apart the mythology and parables and doctrine of different religions in an attempt to intellectualize my way to answers. They have led me back to the spirit of the Old and New Testaments, to the illuminations of the Quaran, to the Chinese belief in Qi, to the Indian Prana, to the spiritual traditions that have existed throughout the centuries. Here I began to find evidence of a life force I was unable to grasp before. It flashes forth constantly, interacting with galaxies and consciousness. Creation continues, over and over, in mind and in matter. It can be found in the mosquito laying eggs in the backwaters of Africa, the stars flaming into existence, the thoughts of a lost child looking for his mother, the mathematician unraveling the theories of existence.

It seems even Einstein, that most famous agnostic, was moved to wonder as evidenced by his words: "Everyone who is seriously involved in the pursuit of science becomes convinced that a spirit is manifest in the laws of the universe—a spirit vastly superior to that of man. . . . In this way the pursuit of science leads to a religious feeling of a special sort . . . quite different from the religiosity of someone more naïve . . ."

In contemplating this life force in her book, *The Quantum Self: Human Nature and Consciousness Defined by the New Physics*, Danah Zohar, a researcher in both physics and religion, asks us to think of God as something embodied within the quantum vacuum and using the laws of physics. This would suggest a God who would, at every moment, be involved in a mutually creative dialogue in the direction of the world. She asks us to consider human beings, you and I, with our physics of consciousness, which mirror the physics of the quantum vacuum, as partners in God's creation!

As such, everything matters.

Part IX

Signs

Chapter 21

Six Days in November
2010

S HE AWOKE THAT MONDAY morning in late November just like every other, polished her optimism with the mindfulness she practiced and bent to the tasks of the day.

She did not know that hours were counting themselves down. She was exquisitely alive to seven that morning, eight, nine, ten, eleven, the turn of the morning to noon. On that Monday after Thanksgiving, she was already preparing for Christmas, weaving greenery through the banister posts and across the mantle of the fireplace. Then it was one, two, three, four, five, six, seven—and she was off to her Italian class—eight, nine, ten—a blood vessel was bursting in her brain. It was the beginning of an end.

THAT SAME MORNING, at 9:00 a.m., I was sitting in a booth at a cozy restaurant, French toast piled on my plate as I ate breakfast with two friends, Sandra and Laura. We met every six months or so to catch up, reconnect and polish some of the rough edges of our lives by sharing them. Around 11:00 a.m., as the empty coffee mugs accumulated on the table, our talk took a turn toward death. *Afraid, not afraid? How could we imagine time existing without us?* Laura told a true story about "not afraid" that happened in 2007 after the death, at age eighty-nine, of her friend, the award-winning, nationally acclaimed author Enid Simmons.*

---

*Names in this piece were changed to protect the privacy of the author.

Laura had been a longtime member of a writing group that Enid facilitated during the eighties and nineties in an upstairs room of an Episcopal convent in Manhattan. Over the years, countless women and a few men met weekly under Enid's motherly wings, which not only caused them to develop as writers but to grow in grace. A few years earlier, Laura brought a gift for Sandra and me to the breakfast meeting. It was a book containing essays by thirty-five former members of Enid's writing groups—groups that had spanned more than forty years. Each essay was a moving and loving testimony to the influence of this woman who enriched the lives of all who wandered into her orbit.

Enid Simmons's public funeral was held at St. John the Divine Cathedral in New York City. Her body was cremated. A few weeks later, a memorial service was held for family and friends in a small country church in Connecticut, where Enid's country home was located. Enid's daughter brought the urn containing her mother's ashes to Connecticut for the service. Afterward, needing to prepare coffee and food for the repast, she asked my breakfast companion, Laura, to keep an eye on the urn for her. Laura, not quite sure what to do with it and knowing she would be nervous carrying the urn around with her during the repast, decided to put it in her car, a little Saab parked on the road nearby the church.

Accompanied by another of Enid's circle of friends, the two women walked from the church to the car. Laura took out her key, pressed the electronic button and unlocked the car. She placed the urn on the floor next to the back seat. Feeling responsible for the safekeeping of such a priceless object, they covered the urn with both their coats as they joked with each other about hiding it.

"Who knows," Laura said, "Enid is a pretty famous author. There might be some one out there just crazy enough to steal her ashes!"

With the urn safely out of sight from prying eyes, Laura pressed the electronic device on her key ring. With the car safely locked, they resumed talking and turned to leave. They had walked only a few yards when they heard the unmistakable sound of the car doors unlocking. Not thinking too much of it, Laura said, "I must have hit the unlock button against my hip while putting the key in my pocket."

She retrieved the key, pointed it toward the car and pressed the lock button again. They heard the locks engage. As they walked away, they heard the click of the doors unlocking again.

"That's strange, I must have done it again," Laura said as she once more extracted the key, pointed it at the car and locked it. This time she mindfully put the key away, making sure she did not inadvertently activate it in her pocket.

But once again, within a few seconds, the sound of the doors unlocking stopped them in their tracks. They turned for the third time, repeated the action, and this time watched the locks engage before turning away. They had walked only a few yards when they heard the sound for the forth time.

"What the heck?"

"Maybe there's something stuck in a door."

Dismayed, they approached the car and proceeded to walk around it, examining the doors to see if something might be caught that prevented the locks from engaging properly. They found nothing amiss.

"Have you been having trouble with the locks?" her friend asked.

"Not before today. I don't know what's going on."

Laura carefully and deliberately pushed the electronic door lock button again. They stood and watched the locks descend into position and waited a minute or two.

All was quiet. "Okay, that should do it," Laura said, as they gingerly turned their backs on the car.

But, no. After walking a few feet with the key still in the palm of her hand, the doors signaled they were unlocking for the fifth time.

"We looked at each other in disbelief," Laura said. "And then, in the same moment, we both knew that my annoying car had suddenly been transformed into something mysterious and wonderful and holy."

Still grasping for a logical explanation but giddy with excitement, they rushed to the car, feeling a new kind of intimacy with their dead friend and an ineffable connection between this world and another.

"Okay, we have to have a little talk with Enid. Obviously she wants our attention and is trying to tell us something."

"I guess she wants us to know she is still around."

They stood in the road and waited a few more minutes as though now that they were prepared, something more would happen. But all was quiet.

"You think she's done?"

"Well, let's find out." Laura pointed her keys at the car and locked it for the sixth time. The two friends waited expectantly. The locks remained engaged. They turned toward the church, haltingly. They listened to the silence behind them, maybe a little disappointed.

Aloud, Laura said, "Anything else, Enid? You certainly got our attention."

Nothing. The Saab stayed locked. It was over. But actually, it was never over. Something inscrutable unlocked in each of them. A Saab that refused to let them go deepened the faith Enid had so eloquently modeled and nurtured in them, and in all the others with whom she came in contact.

THIS WAS NOT ONLY an uplifting story but also one that made the hair stand up on the back of my neck. Monday's breakfast and the conversation's morbid turn toward death ended on a high note. I tucked the story away, like one more arrow in my quiver for defeating doubt. I didn't think of it again until six days later, when the story of Enid's ashes in the Saab unexpectedly came back in a sudden rush of joy.

THE FOLLOWING DAY, Tuesday, I got a call from Ron, my friend Fran's husband. He was crying. He choked out a few sentences. Fran was in the hospital. She came in from her Italian class the previous night, was reading in bed and suddenly began to slur her words. She fell into unconsciousness. Now she was on a respirator and the doctors were giving him little hope for her recovery. "Pray," Ron begged. "We need a miracle."

I WENT TO MASS on Wednesday morning and joined my private prayers with those of Fran's family, who I knew were keeping vigil at her bedside. Her condition hadn't changed. Thursday morning I had an 8:00 a.m. dental appointment that had been scheduled months earlier. I was torn, Mass or dental appointment? Conscientiousness won. When I got to my appointment, the receptionist greeted me with, "Mike's stuck in traffic and won't be here for at least a half hour. Do you want to wait? Or would you like to reschedule?"

The irony of the coincidence wasn't lost on me. I took it as a sign. I quickly rescheduled and drove directly to church. I felt close to my comatose friend as I knelt down and thought, *Okay, Fran, you want me here. Maybe it's to pray for a peaceful passing, maybe to pray for recovery. No matter, I'm here for you.*

Friday morning, I awoke to an email from Ron. Fran was gone. Later that day, with the notice of final arrangements, was a request from Ron, sent to everyone in Fran's electronic mailbox: "Please write your memories of my precious Francesca," for a memorial book he would create. He asked that a copy be brought to the wake or emailed to him.

It felt like too soon and too hard a task, but I knew I would do it.

Since I would be attending Fran's wake late Saturday afternoon, I began to compose my memories of her on Saturday morning. My printer had been balky on Friday and no amount of tinkering with it had gotten it to do its job and print. Now I hoped the balkiness of the previous twenty-four hours had magically straightened itself out. It hadn't. The printer was still dead to all commands. Although what I had written felt very formal and stiff, it was the best I could do. I emailed the piece to Ron and left to attend the wake.

The following morning, Sunday, unable to sleep, I got up early and to take my mind off Fran and her family, I began working on an unrelated project on my computer. After about two hours, the quiet of the morning was broken as the printer started grinding and booting up without any command from me. I watched as it belched and spewed out a few pages. When I went to retrieve them it was "Memories of Fran" that I found in the tray.

I didn't think anything of it. I was just happy the printer was working again. About ten minutes later, my concentration was once again interrupted by a new sound. An incessant *beep beep beep beep beep* broke the silence in the room. Assuming the printer was again self-generating, I got up from the desk to check it, but no, it was quiet. The beeping persisted, more and more irritating by the second. Annoyed, I called to my husband in another room,

"Is that you causing that beeping?"

"No," he said, equally annoyed. "I thought it was you."

We both left our respective computers and followed the unrelenting sound. It seemed to be coming from the kitchen. We shadowed each other around checking the microwave, the oven, the clock, the dishwasher, the coffee machine, everything that had ever been known to beep, even the refrigerator (although that had never been known to beep). Nothing.

"This is weird," I said.

Like detectives, we followed the noise, nervewracking as cicadas in spring, to where the beep was loudest. It seemed to be coming from a drawer where I stored assorted utensils: spatulas, ladles, whisks, the garlic press . . . I opened the drawer. The beeping got louder. We were clearly on the right track. I shuffled the contents of the drawer and picked up a cheese grater, a lemon press, an ice cream scoop, a pizza cutter, and two electronic meat thermometers. The culprit was one of the thermometers, still beeping as I held it in my hand. Baffled, I pressed the red stop button to terminate the offending noise. Quiet blessedly descended. I examined it and tried to figure out what got it going in the drawer on a Sunday morning. I remembered handling it on Thanksgiving, wondering if the batteries were still working as I prepared to cook the turkey. When I realized a heat sensor had already been inserted in the bird, I put the meat thermometer back in the drawer. Now, ten days after Thanksgiving, it was spontaneously beeping?

I couldn't account for it, but no matter. At least I found the source of the annoying noise and stopped it. Bewildered, I laughed, and we both went back to work on our respective computers. Ten minutes later—beeping from the kitchen for a second time. I got up from my desk, walked directly to the kitchen drawer, picked up the thermometer, pressed stop and went back to my work. About twenty minutes later, the quiet was interrupted once again by the chirping meat thermometer.

"Are you kidding me?" I said to no one in particular as I headed for the kitchen. This time my husband followed me.

"Do you think the house is haunted?" I said jokingly as the activity of the self-generating printer, combined with the self-generating meat thermometer, was finally making us both laugh. Yet the word *haunted* caused a free-fall of associations in my mind as I heard myself say it. *Haunted, ghosts, death . . . Fran . . .* With this thought I felt a sudden lightheartedness. Fran, who had remained more present to me in death than when she was a phone call away, now had my attention in a new way.

"This is so strange. Do you think Fran's trying to tell me something?" I asked, half seriously. His eyes were laughing as my husband said, "Maybe, but why would she communicate through a meat thermometer?"

"Good question," I said. "There are a lot of images from which to choose, but a meat thermometer means absolutely nothing to me. Well if it is her, I guess I'll figure it out or it will get revealed someday," I said, dismissing the whole incident as I replaced the meat thermometer in the kitchen drawer for the last time.

At 4:00 p.m. that same Sunday afternoon, I attended a Bach Christmas Concert at the Episcopal Church where Sandra was scheduled to sing. Following the concert, I joined the guests in the community room where coffee and cookies were being served. Here, I unexpectedly found Laura or she found me. We started to talk. I told her about my sorrowful week, my friend Fran's stroke and untimely death. As I spoke, her story of Enid Simmons's memorial service came flooding back. I hadn't thought of it since Monday's breakfast meeting.

Now a light went on. I felt myself resonating in a new way with Laura's experience with the urn, the ashes, and the Saab. Suddenly the two incidents seemed to echo each other. Self-generating door locks with their associated noise that stopped Laura and her friend in their tracks were not dissimilar to the self-generating printer and meat thermometer that stopped me, and my husband, in our tracks that morning.

Now, in what felt like a stunning moment of insight, I felt I knew something I didn't know earlier in the day; the sign wasn't the meat thermometer, it was the beeping!

But what was Fran trying to tell me? Why me? In the hierarchy of her relationships I unquestionably was not one of those counted as her nearest and dearest. Yet, in our Tuesday morning attempts at meditation we often talked about life after death and the way faith was related to that belief. We had struggled together with accepting the inability to know, the living with doubt.

Since Fran's death I was lamenting some missed opportunities to meet and meditate with her. No thought of time running out for us ever entered my mind. I had unwittingly suggested we put our meetings off—I couldn't even remember why. Words from the poet Robert Frost came to me:

> "Knowing how way leads on to way
> I doubt that I shall ever come back"

Now, I thought, *perhaps the beeping is leading me to Enid Simmons, a sign I can go back. Perhaps there's something for me to discover in her writings—something about meditation, about faith, about living with doubt?* I knew very little about her other than she was a famous author and one of Laura's dearest friends. A few years ago, when Laura had given me the book of essays written by Enid's students after her death, I had read Laura's essay, but the others remained unread on my bookshelf.

When I got home from the concert, I removed the book of essays from the shelf. I began to read the tributes to this woman whose life was grounded in spirituality. I read from one of her essayists that Enid Simmons infused her retreats and writing workshops with her sure belief that "death is not the end . . . there is in God's Universe nothing random or pointless, ever; all is part of a grand design."

Many of the essays made reference to the most famous of Enid's sixty published books. *Perhaps I should read it,* I thought.

I started at the library. Sure enough, this award-winning book, published over sixty years ago, was still on the shelf, its pages brimming with the author's magical world of the fifth dimension. It was a place existing beyond imagination, where knowing wasn't limited by space and time, and a shining chasm of Light plus the opportunity to know was found. Here possibility was endless.

One only had to believe.

Chapter 22

The Blue Dress
1990

J O ANN WAS A RELATIVELY new friend. I met her seven years earlier when she married one of my longtime male friends. She was fifteen years younger than I, with smooth young skin, long legs, and a mind like the *Encyclopedia Britannica*, all of which could have been off-putting. But Jo Ann's warmth and humor drew me and everyone else to her.

The night of Jo Ann's mother's wake, I found an empty folding chair set up on the maroon funeral parlor carpet and sat down. After a while, Jo Ann joined me. "I've been waiting for you," she said.

As she lowered herself into a chair, she nodded toward the casket and asked, "Do you recognize the dress my mother is wearing?"

Honestly, I didn't and I told her so. I wondered if maybe I should remember it.

"It's the dress she wore to my wedding. Oh, how she loved it," she said wistfully as she reminisced about how much fun they had shopping for it, traipsing through dress shops in three boroughs of New York to find it.

"She dieted and dropped from a size sixteen to size twelve," Jo Ann said as she turned toward the casket. I followed her gaze to where her mother was laid out amidst a wall of flowers. Her dress, although I could only see part of it in the half closed casket, was sapphire blue. The neckline was a soft cloud of silk draped below her neck, the sleeves sheer and luminous with a trio of pearl buttons at the wrist. The full skirt was set off with a blue satin ribbon sash that culminated in a bow at the waist.

"After the wedding she had the dress shortened so she could wear it again. But that never happened," Jo Ann said sadly. "The weight gradually snuck back up on her, and she never wore the dress again. Until now."

Ah, now I knew why the dress had such importance, why we were talking about it. I had been at the wedding. I might have remembered it. I wished I had.

"I can't believe how fast she went, three months from health to death. "

I knew. It was not long ago that Mama Doris had lugged her baking tins and flan pans to Jo Ann's new loft in Tribeca to help her prepare for her housewarming party. A fabulous dessert maker, an art she had passed down to her daughter, she had been glowing with pride the night of the party as she made herself useful hanging up coats and sharing her secret recipes. There was a touch of the mischievous in her as she rolled her eyes while directing guests into the privacy of the bedroom to meet the gypsy fortune teller her zany daughter had hired to entertain the guests.

Jo Ann had raised her lovely eyebrows at me when I was one of the guests who chose not to visit the gypsy. Not because I didn't believe. The truth was, it made me nervous. It was a no-win situation. I figured God had gotten it right. Not knowing the future was a good thing. If the gypsy had pulled some good news out of her crystal ball, I would have doubted it. If she so much as hesitated or faltered while gazing into her crystal ball, I would have interpreted it as bad news and spent the rest of the night, if not the rest of my life, worrying about it. *No, better leave well enough alone*, I thought.

But no one had seen this coming. There were morphine injections, followed by a ventilator and then restraints to keep Doris from pulling the alien tubes from her throat. Days before her death, the doctors told Jo Ann that her mother would never regain consciousness.

Jo Ann told me how she alternated between praying for a miracle and talking to her mother, even though the doctors had told her she was unconscious. "At first I just begged her to fight, to hang on until we found the right specialist, the right treatment." But then, stumbling as though ashamed, she continued, "Although my tongue could barely form the words, I actually gave her permission to die. I had this feeling she was keeping herself alive for the family—my father, my brothers, and me. It was the hardest thing I ever did, but I told her she could die."

"Do you think she heard you?" I asked.

"Maybe," Jo Ann said. "I asked her for a sign. I hardly knew what I was asking for and it was only later, when something astonishing happened, I even remembered asking."

"What happened?" I asked.

"Not here," she said as she led me to an office and closed the door.

Jo Ann's mother died with the family at her bedside. Later that same day, they all returned to her parents' house. A wake was a foregone conclusion, and there was much to do to accommodate death.

Jo Ann's father, her husband, and her two brothers were downstairs calling family and friends, choosing a casket, selecting a burial plot, calling the church, searching for the insurance policy; the acts that forced the living to keep on when keeping on was the last thing one wanted to do. The women—Jo Ann, her sister-in-law Nancy, and Mrs. Berm, her mother's closest friend—went upstairs to the bedroom to gather clothes to bring to the funeral parlor. Going through Doris's closet, they found the sapphire-blue dress stored in a plastic garment bag. The three women knew immediately this was the dress Doris would choose if she were alive to do the choosing. The weight she had regained after the wedding had evaporated over the previous three months, and it would fit her gloriously again. It had been dry-cleaned, and the extra fabric from shortening it was carefully folded in the bottom of the bag.

It is strange how we the living continue to consult the dead for what would please them. I know after my father died, I spent every weekend of the following spring bucking the traffic to Long Island to prepare the little strip of soil in his backyard for planting his beloved tomatoes. It made me feel close to him.

I totally understood the consensus around the sapphire blue dress.

"But we couldn't find the sash," Jo Ann said. "We turned the bag inside out. It wasn't there, which was weird. I know my mother, and she wouldn't have separated it from the dress.

The missing sash became a cause that overtook the three of them. It was as if her mother would not rest in peace if her belt had gone missing—for eternity. On the one hand, they knew it was irrational, but finding the sash became a symbolic act of love. Doris would want her belt! It was the least they could do for her!

Over the next two hours the three of them rifled through the dresser drawers. They rummaged through plastic containers of out-of-season clothes carefully stored beneath the bed and emptied boxes stored at the top of the closet. They found other belts scattered throughout the closet, carefully threaded onto hangers that held the matching outfits. "Come on, Doris," Mrs. Berm had affectionately mumbled at one point. "We know you didn't get rid of the sash. It's around here somewhere." But it wasn't and they finally gave it up.

As I listened, I could not help but wonder if the mind finds momentary relief from tragedy by focusing on some rote task that allows you to feel like you're doing something, when in reality, there is nothing that can undo the tragedy.

The three women settled on a thin black patent leather belt that belonged with a silk suit. They put it with the dress. They packed a small bag with a silk slip, a gray velvet case with the double strand of pearls and matching earrings that Mama Doris had worn with the dress, a tube of pink lipstick, and her "rosy cheeks" blush. When going through the boxes on top of the closet they had found the sapphire-blue shoes, dyed to match the dress. After hesitating, knowing her mother's feet would not be visible to the mourners who came to kneel at her coffin, Jo Ann added them anyway. She knew her mother would want her shoes. She extracted Doris's wallet from the leather purse carefully placed on a chair the day she went into the hospital for the last time. Inside the wallet was the photograph of her mother at the wedding. Jo Ann removed it from the wallet and placed it on top of the pile. Her mother was out of their hands now. They would give the photograph to some anonymous person at the funeral parlor whose job it was to transform the mask of death back into a semblance of her laughing, loving mother. She could only hope the photo would help him get it right.

Everything in order, they were getting ready to leave the bedroom when there was a soft knock on the door. Mrs. Berm, who was closest, opened it.

"It was my father. He was just standing there. The sapphire-blue sash was in his hand like it was the most ordinary thing in the world."

"Are you looking for this?" he said, extending his hand.

Mrs. Berm saw it first. Then Nancy and I realized what my father was delivering to us.

"Where did you get that?" Nancy shouted as both Mrs. Berm and Jo Ann shrieked from behind her.

At the same moment, the three women's eyes sought each other out and met above the blue ribbon sash cascading like a waterfall from her father's rough hands.

In that fleeting look they shared a knowing, a communion, a comfort beyond all logical explanation. They were, all three of them, laughing now. Sorrow gave way to a giddy joyousness that infused each of them simultaneously. A sudden harmony united them like the first chords of a symphony after all the squeaks and toots of the warm up.

It was Mrs. Berm who put into words what they all were thinking. "Well, I guess Doris does not want that black belt spoiling her beautiful dress."

By now Jo Ann's two brothers and her husband came running up the stairs to see what was the matter, what all the shouting and laughing was about.

Looking shocked and baffled by the barrage and variety of "Where did you get that?" questions being thrown at him, the new widower answered earnestly. "I found it in the piano bench."

"The piano bench! What even made you look for it in the piano bench?"

"I wasn't looking for it."

"Then why did you go to the piano bench?"

"I don't know," he said thoughtfully as he explained how his sons kept insisting he sit down and try to rest. Just to get them off his back, not because he wanted to, he sat down in his lounge chair in the living room, the others trailing him there.

"I couldn't get comfortable. I was about to push back in the chair and put my feet up when I just got this idea to check the piano bench. When I saw the sash, I knew it didn't belong there. Then I remembered the blue dress from the wedding and thought you might need it."

Jo Ann looked at her husband and brothers as if in disbelief. "That's exactly what happened," her brother John said, hardly able to contain his own amazement. "We were all in the same room, and Dad just got up and walked over to the piano bench without saying a word to any of us. He started moving the sheet music around. I thought maybe he was looking for some music he wanted for the funeral. Then he headed upstairs."

Giddy as infatuated schoolgirls, the three women, all talking at once, tried to explain to this confused widower how their search for the sash had ended in failure and how his visit to the room was bringing them so much more than the sapphire ribbon he was offering them.

A smile grew in and around her father's eyes. The pain from Doris's death momentarily receded. Her presence filled the room, and the blue satin sash spoke, like a dream that wasn't a dream, to all of them.

MANY OF THOSE WHO shared their stories with me, having had a spontaneous experience of presence, want to recreate it. And yet, as stated earlier, such experiences can't be induced or generated by will. Yet mediums offer an opportunity to pursue another whiff of communication.

Unbeknownst to Jo Ann, it was a yearning to re-create his mother's presence that sent John, her oldest brother, to a medium. Many years later, Jo Ann got an unusual call from him. She was living in Georgia by this time, having moved from the New York area a few years after her mother died. John told his sister that he had been to a medium. He was confused by the message he received. It was about silver molds for making chocolate. The medium insisted it was a clear message from Doris. "Have you any idea what this could mean?" he asked his sister.

Jo Ann laughed. She was baffled. Silver chocolate molds? Then suddenly the light went on in her memory. Doris had once worked in a candy making plant and had salvaged molds when the business closed. Her mother had given them to her, the only girl in the family, when she was first married. Jo Ann never had an inclination to make candy so she just stored the cardboard box that contained the pans in the basement along with other sentimental but useless items. Yet when she moved, she could not bring herself to get rid of them. She packed them but never even unpacked the box. It was still stored in her basement. She headed for the basement while still on the phone with her brother and tore open the box. Not quite silver, the molds were tin! Old and battered tin pans for making chocolate candy their mother worked with before they were born. But at that moment they were more precious than gold, as sister and brother shared a surge of love coming at them from—from where? They couldn't name it, but knew what they knew—and that was enough.

Chapter 23

Tina's Story
THE LETTER

T INA, A PROFESSIONAL woman in her early fifties, shared her experience around the death of her mother. Tina and her mother lived across the country from each other. Tina would visit when she could, but it fell to her sister to do most of the caretaking during her mother's illness. Confined to a wheel-chair and unable to walk in the months prior to her death, the mother's condition steadily deteriorated. There had been a family reunion a few years prior that her mother had attended in spite of her poor health. Before her death, she insisted she was going to go to Florida for a reunion planned for the following spring. Tina and her sister knew there was no way that was going to happen, but they let their mother enjoy her fantasy.

As anticipated, she died. A few months later in the spring, the rest of the family flew to Florida for the planned reunion. Tina and her husband were staying at a hotel. Upon returning to their room one night, they both noticed a folded piece of paper lying on top of a built-in bureau that extended along one side of the room. The maid had meticulously cleaned the room. That one piece of paper was the only object that seemed out of place. Assuming it was some kind of a communication from the hotel about the bill or their stay in the room, her husband picked it up and read it. His face drained of color as he turned to Tina and handed her the piece of paper like a hot potato. "It's a letter from your mother," he said.

Tina looked at the page and immediately recognized the handwriting. It was her mother's handwriting! With her heart beating wildly, she read:

> Dear Tina,
> I just wanted to let you know how proud I am of you and what a good daughter you have always been.
> Love,
> Mom

Tina remembers gasping. She had never seen the note before, couldn't imagine how it appeared in the room. She was confused, disoriented, and filled with a sudden surge of happiness as she felt her mother's presence. She and her husband huddled over the letter, trying to figure out how it came to be lying out in the open in a hotel room in Florida. When she had calmed down enough to speak Tina found herself laughing out loud and saying, "Well, Mom said she was coming to the reunion, and she's letting me know she's here."

Tina quickly called her sister and the rest of the family, who came rushing to her room to examine and read the letter that had seemed to materialize out of thin air. The whole family was uplifted. Her mother's presence rippled through each of them.

By the next day, Tina was trying to account for the whole incident in a rational way. Perhaps her mother had slipped the note into her pocketbook months before when she was visiting her in California. If that had happened, it went unnoticed in her pocketbook during all the intervening months. Had it somehow slipped out of her bag during the reunion and wound up someplace in the room where a maid found it and placed it where Tina could not miss it? The scene she rationalized was probably within the realm of possibility. But it didn't matter. The excitement of receiving the letter, written who knows when and never before read, produced a joy that would never diminish. Tina and her sisters, elated, welcomed their mother to the reunion. They had no doubt she was with them.

Chapter 24

Eileen's Story
THE NOTRE DAME INFLUENCE

"Faith: For those who believe, no explanation is necessary; for those who don't, no explanation is possible." Anonymous

ILEEN AND HER HUSBAND, Hank, knew his death was imminent. They were preparing as best they could for her life without him. They agreed that she would sell their big house, where they had raised their six children, within a year of his passing and buy a smaller one. A few days before he died, Eileen asked Hank, "After you're gone, will you send me some kind, any kind, of message so I know you can hear me, that you're near?"

Hank answered, "I don't know how that works, but I'll try."

Hank died on November 15, 2012. Although she wasn't planning to put their house on the market until spring, Eileen was anxious to get an idea of what was available in smaller homes. On December 8, three weeks after Hank's death, she set out with a real estate agent who showed her five or six homes. None of them even piqued her interest. Ready to go home after a long day, the agent suggested they look at "one more." A ranch on a pretty winding street with a secluded backyard surrounded by woods, it excited Eileen. Everything told her this was the house for her. She didn't want to lose it by waiting.

During their marriage, Hank and Eileen had made all the big decisions together. Before he died, they had agreed that there was no reason for her to rush into selling the house. Now, seeing this ranch and loving it was so unexpected and confusing.

She went back the next day, Saturday, to take another look.

"On my second visit I noticed the painting above the fireplace," Eileen told me. "It was *The Four Horsemen of Notre Dame*, Knute Rockney's legendary 1924 team. I hadn't noticed it the day before, and I started to fill up with tears when I recognized the painting that was hanging so prominently in the room. Hank was an avid Notre Dame football fan and would often stop in South Bend when traveling. He loved the school, the campus, the history of it all, and especially the football team. As the owner noticed my sudden tearfulness, he looked at me quizzically. He didn't know what to say. Feeling I owed him an explanation, I told him of Hank's recent death and of his love for Notre Dame.

"When I finished, he started to smile and told me his real estate agent had suggested he remove the painting while showing the house, exchange it for a more neutral picture.

"'I took her advice on most everything else, but not about the painting,' he said. 'My son graduated from Notre Dame and I have a strong connection to the school. Now I know why I left it there.'"

As she listened, Eileen remembered asking Hank for a sign before he died, and again the previous night as she wrestled with trying to make a decision without him. The power of the coincidence was not lost on her. But still she waited.

Eileen visited the house again the next morning for the third time and made the commitment to buy it.

"That night I listed my house with the same agent. It went on the market Monday morning, and by early afternoon I had a full-price offer with a requested closing date of January 31. Agents on all sides were astounded. To see two real estate deals come together so seamlessly within four days, to sell a house in this terrible market in less than twenty-four hours was unheard of."

The holidays came in a blur of grief, but then on Christmas Day another coincidence. Eileen told me that Hank's favorite part of Christmas dinner at their son Steve's house had always been black coffee and Sambuca served at the end of the meal with their daughter Kim's cookies. Earlier that afternoon, Steve had hooked up his iPod to his stereo. He told his mother later that he had over four thousand songs on that iPod, and he shuffled them in no particular order before Christmas dinner. As Steve began to pour coffee and pass the Christmas cookies, the Notre Dame fight song came soaring out of the speakers. "Conversation just stopped," Eileen said. "We all looked at each other and began to laugh and cry and agree that Dad was right here with us, right then. Steve told us he had no memory of even putting that fight song on his iPod, yet there it was, at that particular moment, loud and clear."

On Friday, January 27, fifteen hours before Eileen was to move out of the house, bad news. Her buyer's mortgage application had been denied. The deal was off. The next morning the agent started showing the house again. Once again, within twenty-four hours, there were two verbal, over-list-price offers.

One offer was $10,000 more than the other with a closing on February 28. This buyer was a colleague of a neighbor who claimed to have always admired the house. He really wanted the house, but his insistence on re-doing all of the inspections was time consuming and "a pain," as Eileen put it. The family who made the lesser offer was a job-transferred couple, currently living with their son in a Residence Inn. They were desperate for a home.

"While trying to fall asleep, I thought of Hank, and again wondered what he would want me to do? *How about sending me another message or sign*, I thought.

"I was still waiting for the written offers to come through a few days later, while walking past a store's Valentine Day display. I started reminiscing. February fourteenth was the anniversary of my very first date with Hank. This would be the first time in forty-two years I wouldn't receive a Valentine from him."

That evening, the agent delivered a packet containing the written offer from the second family. It included a letter the couple wrote after touring the house again that afternoon. "I didn't open the envelope, just put it down on the kitchen table and listened to my agent's verbal explanation of what it contained," Eileen said. "The agent left at 10:00 p.m. and I was tired. I just left the offer on the table, showered and went to bed. The following morning, I opened the envelope to read through the letter and the offer. I still didn't know which offer to take. Then I glanced at the signatures on the bottom of the last page.

"Bill and Cheryl Valentine."

"I didn't have to ask the question anymore. Needless to say, Hank's Valentine trumped $10,000. That day I told the Valentines they had the house."

Chapter 25

Nicole's Story
THE SONG

NICOLE WAS ONE of the two partners who owned and operated a busy beauty salon in a cosmopolitan town in New Jersey. I got to know her professionally over the eight years she cut and styled my hair.

We often shared stories while she snipped and shaped. Nicole was young enough to be my daughter and so our stories generally reflected the generation gap. They were mostly about family and holidays, who was cooking, who was visiting. There were twins in my family, and her mother was a twin. We discussed the bonding of twins, how close her mother remained to her twin sister, Rae, until her mother died when Nicole was twenty-six years old.

"My mother was a nervous wreck her whole life," Nicole told me. "She was afraid to let me or my sisters out of her sight. Aunt Rae always knew when my mother was worried and would try to get her to calm down, worry less. There was a song, 'I Hope You Dance,' that was like a code between them. My aunt would sing it to my mother, and my mother would smile and get calm. It was some magical twin thing that my father and my sisters and brother and I all knew about and loved."

When Nicole's brother got married shortly after their mother's death, he asked Aunt Rae to dance with him at the wedding reception. "The song my brother chose was 'I Hope You Dance.'"

"Mom will be on the dance floor with us," he said to Aunt Rae.

Although I was of the same generation as Nicole's mother, I didn't recognize the song.

"I'm sure you've heard it," Nicole said. Then, glancing around the salon, to be sure no one else was paying attention to us, she began to sing the chorus very softly:

> I hope you still feel small when you stand beside the ocean
> Whenever one door closes I hope one more opens
> Promise me that you'll give faith a fighting chance
> And when you get the choice to sit it out or dance
> Dance
> I hope you dance . . .

Her impromptu performance confirmed that even though the song had been very popular, I had never heard it.

As Nicole bent in front of me to align the length of my hair under each of my ears I asked, "Are you like your mother?"

"No, thank God," she said. "After seeing how stressed she was all the time, and how hard that made it for me and my sisters, I vowed to be different."

"Is your aunt like a second mother to you now?" I asked.

"No," Nicole said, "my mother died in July of 2001, and in September Aunt Rae was diagnosed with pancreatic cancer. She, too, died within the year."

When Nicole became pregnant in 2009, she continued with her usual breakneck pace at the salon. The pregnancy was going fine. But early in her sixth month, she started to stain. Reasonably alarmed, she went to the doctor who told her, "Get off your feet for a few days." His confidence that the staining would subside allayed her fears. I learned of this at the time because my appointment was shifted to her partner.

She was back in the salon two weeks later, joyful that the scare turned out to be a temporary glitch in her pregnancy.

The following week I got a call from the salon. Something had gone very wrong. Nicole was not going to be back until after she gave birth. She was to be on total bed rest for the rest of her pregnancy. There were no details, just grave concern that continued throughout the next three months. And then one day I walked into the salon to find it bedecked with balloons and streamers and a huge pink poster that read, "IT'S A GIRL." Three months later the new mom was back on the job.

I would not know details of what happened until almost five years had gone by. By that time Nicole had given birth, without incident, to her second child, a son. In the context of talking about my writing this book, Nicole asked, "Did I ever tell you what happened to me the day my daughter was born?"

She hadn't. She stopped cutting my hair, as she got ready to revisit the day. Pointing to her wrist and forearm, she said, "Look, I get goose flesh just thinking about it." and sure enough, I could see the tiny bumps coating her arm. I watched her shiver as she began.

"After I was put on total bed rest in my sixth month, I was in and out of the hospital eight times for bleeding. The doctor was trying to get me to the thirty-eighth week, when the baby would have the best chance for a healthy survival. With that last bleeding episode, during my thirty-seventh week, they kept me at the hospital. I was there less than two days when suddenly I started to hemorrhage.

"It was horrible," she said. "There was blood everywhere. The bed was saturated. I thought my baby was gone, could not possibly still be alive inside me with so much blood draining from my body. I was so frightened. I panicked. I couldn't breathe. I was screaming, 'Give me something, and make it stop.' An emergency C-section was ordered. An anesthesiologist came to me. Nurses rushed me to the delivery room. After not taking so much as an aspirin for all those months, I wanted something, anything to calm me down. I wanted to be knocked out, my consciousness obliterated. I didn't want to face what was going on. I didn't want to know what was happening. The anesthesiologist told me he couldn't give me anything. I continued to holler and cry as I gasped for breath. 'Give me something, anything . . . make it all stop . . . make this nightmare go away.' I was out of control and couldn't help myself.

"The nurses and anesthesiologist escorted my bed out of the room, down the hallway, onto the elevator, off the elevator, down another hallway , all the while trying to talk me down. As we approached the delivery room, the double doors swung open, and as they did, I heard the words and music of 'I Hope you Dance.' It was being piped through the sound system in the delivery room and filled the air like a breeze in the desert. In that instant, I knew my mother was with me. Panic left. I could breathe again. I stopped crying and became controlled. There was no doubt in my belief. My mother was there. She was making herself known through the music. She was letting me know she was there to take care of her grandchild and me.

"The nurses who were each holding one of my hands, probably to keep me from lunging from the bed in my panic, both noticed it. 'What just happened to you?' one of them said. Then the other, her face bent close to mine, said, 'What's going on? Something just happened. You're not the same person as you were a minute ago.'

"But I couldn't tell them what happened. I hardly knew, myself. How could I explain that my dead mother was in that room with me?

"I just said, 'I' m okay. You can let go now.'

"And they let go their grip on my hands. I was safe with my mother.

"After the birth I couldn't stop gushing to my father and sisters and brother, 'It was Mommy, it was Mommy, she was there, and she got me through.'

"And this is the strange thing: in my family, to this day, we never talk about my mother. I don't really know why. I think it's just too painful for any of us to go there. She was sick for nine horrible years. We were all teenagers, and it was such a long awful time. It's an unspoken rule we don't break. No one brings her up. But that day I broke the unwritten rule. I wanted my sisters, my brother, my father to know that Mommy was with me. And no one doubted that she was as we laughed and cried and remembered her together."

Chapter 26

Janice's Story
BLUE LIGHT

On Memorial Day weekend, the first big weekend of the summer, Andrea's summer was about to end, although she did not know it at the time. Chatting happily on the phone with her mother, Janice, excited about the upcoming summer, Andrea said, "I just have to take a shower, and I'll be off to the beach house. I already filled the car with gas, shopped for a lobster pot and a new bathing suit. I'm all packed. Got coffee, eggs, yogurt, sheets, an extra pillow, towels, *Vogue* and *Time Magazine*. I can't wait to get to the shore."

"Have fun," Janice said. "I'll talk to you next week." Twenty minutes later, Janice's phone rang again, "Mom, I found a lump in my breast while I was taking my shower."

A whirlwind week of doctor's appointments, mammograms, and biopsies followed. Finally a diagnosis—malignant breast cancer. As the family absorbed the implications of the diagnosis, Janice glimpsed the future. She wanted to strike a bargain with fate, take that lump and all that was to come, the surgery, chemotherapy, nausea, weight loss, radiation, fatigue, and genetic testing and make it her own. She wanted to send her daughter to the beach instead. As powerless as she had ever been, she prayed, welding prayers of petition for her daughter's health and prayers of thanksgiving when Andrea got through one more day.

God, science, and a rose quartz heart were the three legs of an altar mother and daughter constructed to bear the weight of a cure for Andrea's cancer.

Andrea's friend Cathy had given her the rose quartz. They had been little girls, only eleven years old, when Cathy's father gave his daughter a rose quartz heart a few days after she was diagnosed with multiple sclerosis. Known in legend for its healing power and divine energy, Cathy wore it fastened to a gold chain around her neck. She vowed never to take it off. When she was fifteen, she learned her multiple sclerosis was in remission. A few months later, the rose quartz heart broke in two. Although she could no longer wear it, she treasured the two halves and always knew exactly where they were. Over the next twenty-five years, she transferred the pieces from her teenage jewelry box through a series of velvet cases to the one in the bedroom she now shared with her husband. The two halves, carefully wrapped in tissue paper, were Cathy's insurance policy, a talisman to hold on to if ever she needed it again. The day after Andrea told her about her breast cancer, Cathy unwrapped one half of the broken rose quartz heart and carried it to her friend.

"Take this," she said to Andrea. "I beat multiple sclerosis, and you'll beat cancer."

"I'm going to wear it in my bra, next to my heart," Andrea said. And that is where it remained for the next year and a half.

By the summer of 2008, whether from treatments, prayer, or the rose quartz, her cancer was in remission. Andrea went back to work, bought a new condominium, adopted a cat, and invested in a new wardrobe. She rejoined the beach house with the friends, who had saved her spot when she was forced to drop out the previous summer.

As summer ended, headaches sent Andrea to the doctor. Within a few weeks the diagnosis of a sinus infection morphed into tumors in her brain. More chemo, more radiation. The cancer was unrelenting. Andrea died on February 20, 2009, less than two years from that moment before the moment, when the summer and her life still stretched in front of her without a wrinkle.

All through the previous months, hope had bobbed within Janice like a cork in an ocean of fear. Now there was nothing left to hope for. She returned the rose quartz to Cathy. Her desire to go on was dead, lying in the casket with her daughter.

Yet it would be Andrea who, in the end, showed Janice the way to the rest of her life.

Shortly after Andrea's death and before the funeral, Janice was standing beside her bed. "As I turned, I saw an amorphous hand and arm reaching out towards me. It was clothed in a flowing sleeve and bathed in blue light. I reached for it but couldn't grasp it. I had this immediate intuition it was Andrea, trying to reach me, letting me know something survives death."

Janice continued. "I also knew I could be hallucinating, that grief can make you crazy. Nothing like this had ever happened to me before, but even as it struck me that I might be losing my mind, I felt an intense up-rush of peace, a sense that Andrea was in the room with me."

"It was similar to the way I felt after waiting for her to come home at night when she was a teenager and finally hearing the car door slam or the refrigerator being opened in the middle of the night and knowing, by the familiar sound, that she was safe. It was unlike the need to have her present in the flesh, to see and touch and hold. Rather it was a letting go of that need in order to accept the momentary sense of Andrea's presence in a way I can't explain."

Janice clung to the image. She tried to recreate it, test whether shifting light, shadows, her imagination, or something electrical in the room had caused it. She took the same posture alongside the bed, turned her head the same way, over and over again.

"I couldn't reproduce it," she said, "but the feeling that it was a sign from Andrea got stronger and stronger. I asked myself, why a disembodied arm, clothed in a flowing sleeve, bathed in blue light? Of all the images in this creation, why would Andrea come to me as a disembodied arm? And if it wasn't a sign from her, why did I feel such relief and peace while it was happening?"

The answer was embedded in the question. In the weeks before her death, Andrea's cancer had spread to her spine. While in the hospital she was unable to lift her arms or her legs to turn over in bed. She kept repeating, as if to convince her parents, "My limbs are not my real arms and legs. My actual limbs are under the bed and the ones attached are just wooden facsimiles. I'm actually floating above the bed, and my real arms and legs are attached to my real body."

"To hear this coming from your child was one of the most painful experiences of those last weeks," Janice said.

As I listened to the horror of my friend's experience in her daughter's hospital room, I thought of the many trauma patients I worked with over the years in my role as a psychotherapist. Such experiences were not unheard of and were often seen in people with post traumatic stress disorder, as rape victims and accident victims reported observing the scene of their own trauma from outside their bodies. In a creative act of dissociation, the mind separates itself from the body in order to bear the unbearable. In doing so, the trauma victim becomes a bystander to the physical or emotional pain being inflicted on her body. A stunning defense, dissociation is a capacity to alter reality in order to survive it.

As we spoke, the disembodied arm and hand bathed in light suddenly overflowed with meaning for Janice. It was the image of a transformed limb. In the context of her very intimate and powerful shared experience with Andrea while she was dying, it communicated so much. Although it was not within Janice's power or the realm of reality to touch or grasp the hand, it had been offered, and that was everything. Janice had told no one about the experience. But she held it close, her touchstone as her world dissolved around her.

At the wake on the day following Janice's experience, Cathy came to Janice and pressed the recently returned half of the rose quart heart into her hand. "I want you to have this," she said.

A few months after her death, Andrea's friends organized a fundraising event for the Young Cancer Survivors Group in honor of Andrea. Fifty baskets were donated and were to be raffled off. Janice planned to contribute three, one with wine and cheese, another with note and wrapping paper, and the third with baby items. One of Andrea's beach housemates was pregnant, and Janice secretly hoped this woman would win the baby basket.

"I had all the items but just could not bring myself to work on the baskets. The day before the event, I pushed myself to assemble them. As I removed the price tag from a new basket, scissors in one hand, the tag in the other, I was stunned. There on a rectangle of white linen sewn into the side of the basket was a label—and stitched into it with blue thread I saw *Baskets by Andrea*. My heart lifted in my chest. Out of the dozens of baskets I considered, I bought one with Andrea's name inscribed in it, unbeknownst to me until then. And then another coincidence: the next day at the raffle, Andrea's pregnant housemate won the basket."

Janice told me of two other instances, when images of light came unbidden and spoke to her of Andrea's presence. The first took place in September, seven months after Andrea's death. It had little meaning at the time but took on significance months later.

"I was in the bedroom," Janice said, "when I saw multiple small sunbursts of light out of the corner of my eye. It happened a couple of times over a two-day period, always in the bedroom. There was no feeling of comfort associated with the light flashes, like the rush of peace I felt when I saw the amorphous arm clothed in blue light after Andrea's death. These sunbursts scared me. I thought I might have a detached retina. The ophthalmologist examined my eyes but could find nothing wrong and no evidence of light bursts. Relieved, I put it out of my mind."

The second incident took place on May 8 of the next year, Janice's birthday and the day after Mother's Day. As Janice lay on her bed, unable to sleep, she prayed to her daughter. *If possible, please come to me in my dreams as a gift for my birthday and Mother's Day.* At some point, as she lay there, images slowly began to appear.

"I saw blue twinkles against a dark-blue glowing background and a white vaporous form rapidly darting around, sometimes appearing to be reaching out, and at times separating in a way. Then an oval appeared, which seemed to be a featureless face."

This imagery filled her with comfort. Although the blue twinkles were different from the starbursts that sent her running to the ophthalmologist months earlier, the realization that both experiences were forms of moving light grasped her. In retrospect, she came to believe the starbursts were a sign she was unable to interpret until her birthday when she called to her daughter, and Andrea answered through images of light.

As we spoke, I asked Janice if she had any idea why these experiences happened only in her bedroom.

"I've thought about that," she said, "and I can only come up with one thing. During the months when Andrea was going for cancer treatments, she would often stop by the house in the late afternoon on her way home. Although she didn't live with us, she had her own key. If the house was quiet, she made her way to the bedroom. She knew that, as the day wound down, her father went to the den and tried to doze in his lounge chair, and I went into the bedroom to read before getting on with dinner. But it was in the bedroom where Andrea knew she would find me."

No sooner had those words fallen upon both our ears than we found ourselves smiling. Once again, Janice's own words answered the question she had been pondering. Like faith, believing in signs was a leap into the unknown.

For those like Janice and others who experience imagery, it is the enduring comfort the images produce, a comfort that touches the deepest parts of their being that bears the weight of their belief in a sign of post-mortem survival.

To reject that comfort is to foreclose on possibility; to embrace it is to dwell in possibility and be open to whatever the universe, in all its hidden abundance, offers from its infinite source.

Addendum:

Cathy's father died around the same time as Andrea. Cathy visited a medium. During the session, the medium told Cathy she had a message for her. It was to thank her for what she did for Andrea's mother.

Part X

Tying It All Together:

The Interface of Faith, Science, and Personal Experience

Chapter 27

Light

"When science sees consciousness to ba a fundamental quality of reality, and religion takes God to be the light of consciousness shining within us all, the two world views start to converge."
Peter Russell

THERE IS A BEAUTIFUL ancient Sanskrit greeting still in use among Hindus—*Namaste*, which means, "the Spirit in me bows to the Spirit in you." In using this greeting, there is the implicit understanding we are all part of the one divine spirit. Now science is affirming this ancient intuition, as evidence of an underlying oneness connecting us all emerges from the discoveries of quantum science.

Light is the common image shared by the world's great religions. It is used to depict transcendence and the spirit of the inexpressible mystery surrounding creation and immortality. One only has to examine the art and icons associated with both Eastern and Western faith communities to find the spiritual and holy represented by haloes and auras and rays of radiance. References to light to speak about and depict the holy and the spiritual are also found in the sacred texts of the world's great religions preserved and passed down through the ages.

Light is also associated with the introversive mystical state of consciousness. It is one of the defining marks of cosmic consciousness. It can be found in the writings and art of all religions in attempts to describe mystical experiences. It has led to the speculation that intellectual or spiritual illumination and enlightenment may be something more than a metaphor.

Science also has a lot to say about light. It has been scientifically established that there are photons—particles of light—in every atom in the universe, including the matter that composes you and me. Although mystics have long referred to us as beings of light, it is only now quantum science is supporting and validating this premise, intuited for centuries, and long woven into the subtext of spiritual practice.

The physicist Peter Russell writes, "Physical light has no mass and is not part of the material world. The same is true of consciousness; it is immaterial." Like light, consciousness has no place and no shape; unimpeded by time and space, it is invisible, yet illuminates everything. We see this played out constantly—say in the moment you become conscious of falling in love or falling out of love, or the moment you solve a problem, be it some obscure mathematical equation or simply in finding the right word for a crossword puzzle. These are eureka moments containing a before and after, made possible by individual consciousness. The moment light floods the dark, we know something in a new way.

We have learned that physical light is fundamental to the universe. Without it, the earth's temperature would plummet hundreds of degrees. Our bodies would go cold as we and everything else became hard, frozen dust. Peter Russell tells a parallel truth, "The light of consciousness is likewise fundamental; without it there would be no experience. . . ." Consciousness at its most basic is frozen light.

Not coincidentally, light has come to be associated with death in a concrete way. Near-death experiences are replete with images of light, as are actual death experiences. Studies verify that dying organisms emit intense amounts of light. This emission is called a "light shout," and it is more than a thousand times greater than a person's usual resting state. Some can actually see it.

It is not a hallucination. On rare occasions, people have reported seeing this light radiating from a dying person, in spite of the fact that they did not know the person was dying.

Since matter can be transformed into energy and energy transformed into light, the theologian Cletus Wessels proposed a stunning idea in *Jesus in the New Universe Story*. He suggested that, just as the body recycles completely every seven years, replacing all its cells and matter, and yet the person remains the same, so too, the make-up of the body after death may be composed of matter, energy, or light while retaining its identity and transcending space and time.

Stories of light connected with death led the theologian Barbara Fiand, writing in *In the Stillness You Will Know*, to speculate: since light seems to be the basic primordial reality of the universe, and matter (frozen light) and energy (light) are interchangeable, perhaps our bodies are simply light's radiation locus (or frequency) while we are here on earth. She asks us to consider if the light of which we are made simply moves on at a time of our physical death—moves out of our body into the universe.

The door to a new and exciting faith perspective opened for me upon reading Fiand's report of the Rainbow Body Phenomenon associated with death in the Tibetan culture. Writing in *From Religion Back to Faith*, she chronicles stories about the corpses of highly developed spiritual individuals vanishing within days of death. It is said that often rainbows appear in the sky during and subsequent to the dying process as the body of the saintly man is absorbed into the light."

Fiand tells of a Buddhist meditation master, one such saintly man known for extraordinary compassion, who asked that upon his death his body not be buried for eight days. His request was honored. It was observed that, as each day progressed, his body seemed to be shrinking. On the eighth day his body vanished.

In 2002, a Benedictine brother, David Steindl-Rast, became interested in these stories because they touched the roots of his faith in the resurrection of Jesus, a man of deep compassion whose body vanished shortly after his entombment and appeared to his followers afterwards.

This is a sentence that touched the roots of my own faith. Here was an avenue to reconciling the core belief of Christianity, the resurrection, with an afterlife and immortality for all people. The exclusivity of one faith over another dissipated in the light that now seemed to belong to all.

Steindl-Rast points out that in today's world, the resurrection of Jesus Christ is interpreted differently, depending on one's spiritual leanings. For fundamentalists, the resurrection—the act of rising from the dead—happened only to Jesus and couldn't happen to any other human. The minimalists, on the other hand, focus on Jesus' spirit living on, and believe the resurrection had less to do with his body.

Open to the concept that the body, too, is significant in the spiritual realm, and that certain spiritual experiences are universal, Steindl-Rast enlisted the help of a Roman Catholic priest familiar with the Tibetan culture and language, Father Francis Tiso. They traveled together to Tibet to investigate the Rainbow Body Phenomenon.

Interviews conducted with eyewitnesses and Tibetan masters led the two men to document the case of Khenpo A-chos, a Gelugpa monk known for his holiness. According to eyewitnesses, a few days before the monk died, a rainbow appeared directly above his hut. After his death, dozens of rainbows appeared in the sky. After seven days, his body, which had been wrapped in a yellow cloth, had completely vanished. It was reported that he appeared in visions to another lama and other individuals after the death. Their research also found documentation from centuries ago of bodies shrinking or disappearing after death, as well as represented in the ancient art associated with Buddhism.

IS THIS HOW WE SURVIVE, as waves of personality resonating in the light of the spheres? Is immortality built into natural law the way consciousness seems to extend beyond the brain in a kind of omnipresence? In the quantum world, where time and space do not exist, will the wave pattern that is each one of us be incorporated into all that is to come, just as it is part of the present and was a part of the past? These questions will probably never be answered in our time- and space-bound universe. Science, constrained by its inability to subtract the act of influencing an observation by the very act of measuring it, hasn't and may never prove God. Yet it has opened a window for me into the hidden reality of a cosmic consciousness where all things seem possible, if not provable. With wonder I can approach the spiritual traditions of the rainbow body, the scientific discoveries of the body, consciousness as light, and the belief in an afterlife as being interrelated.

No religion requires one to believe any aspect of psychic phenomenon or non-local consciousness or any aspect of quantum physics from which these speculations arise. Religion does just fine without the physical sciences. Yet my own spiritual journey has been gifted with a quantum leap forward, as it were, as science and theology offer fresh ways of apprehending the spiritual that finds its expression in our individual consciousness. My personal experiences of presence, coincidence, and prayer, which seem to stretch beyond the limits of time and space, have enriched my faith. They have enhanced my belief in the afterlife and validated my belief in an immortal (transcendent) soul for all people, for all time.

Chapter 28

Flatlands to Fields:
STRETCHING THE MIND TO SEE

"God is the field–the dynamic energy field of Inter-Being–in which we live and move and have our being."   Paul Knitter

THE SPIRITUAL WORLD has always alluded to connections emanating from outside of time. I think of my sense of my father's presence as the glass fell out of the light fixture hours after I cleaned his workroom, of a letter written by a woman before her death that surfaced in a hotel room for her daughter to find months later, a favorite song bursting forth over speakers in the delivery room in a moment of crisis, a Valentine delivered at just the right moment for making a crucial decision, flowers blossoming in startling circumstances, a two-week-old helium-filled yellow smiley-face balloon found perched on a dead son's pillow. To a bystander, these events would have gathered little or no notice; they were devoid of meaning. Yet for those involved, because of previously shared intimate experiences and connection with the dead around the objects involved, the "coincidences" were imbued with symbolic and spiritual significance. Jung called these events synchronicities. Others call them simply coincidences, while others call them Divine Providence.

It is difficult, if not impossible, to find an image to depict consciousness operating beyond the brain. In the course of writing these pages I came across the work of Edwin Abbot, who made concrete the abstract notion of other dimensions, offering a model for apprehending what can't be detected by the five senses.

In 1884, in his novella *Flatlands*, Abbot wrote of a two-dimensional world, a fantasy reality where there was only length and width, no depth. He asks the reader to imagine what such a world would be like—people would be pressed flat on a flat world, like in a picture book. Then he suggests a visit by a three-dimensional creature and asks if that creature could be perceived in a two-dimensional reality. The answer is "no." It would not be perceived. It might be experienced as a dot or a line but the third dimension, depth, could never be accessed. It would remain invisible, ineffable, unexplainable.

The concept was so unimaginable that *Flatlands* was basically ignored when it was first published. It was rediscovered in 1920 after Einstein published his special theory of relativity, which introduced the concept of time as the fourth dimension. Accordingly, we live, breathe and exist in a four-dimensional space-time continuum. According to Gary Zukav, writing in *The Dancing Wu Li Masters: An Overview of the New Physics*, "If we could view reality in the space-time continuum of Einstein's special theory of relativity, we would see everything that now seems to unfold before us with the passing of time (and also everything that we consider past) . . . exists in toto, painted, as it were, on the fabric of space-time. We would see all, the past, the present and the future with one glance."

This seems to imply, just as the inhabitants of *Flatlands* were able to perceive only length and width and unable to experience depth, perhaps we as humans are also limited in our ability to experience time as a dimension.

Alluding to other dimensions from the scientific perspective is the physicist David Bohm, who writes in *Wholeness and the Implicate Order*, "We have seen that in the 'quantum' context, the order in every immediately perceptible aspect of the world is to be regarded as coming out of a more comprehensive Implicate Order, in which all aspects ultimately merge . . ."

Now science is offering us new ways to approach the intuitions that have filled human hearts with a sense of "the more" since consciousness first erupted on the planet. It is to be found in the writings of the mystics and others who try to convey the power of a transcendent experience.

I wonder if there is anyone alive, mystic or not, who does not resonate with this desire for wholeness. In my own life, I have seen it played out in the myriad ways of the world—a search for love, that consciousness of belonging to or being united with another, the desire for material possessions, status, recognition. All offer a temporary sense of wholeness. Always this inching up the ladder for more, only to find it doesn't endure. There is always another "more" to ignite the smoldering ashes of desire.

Some suggest this need for worldly wholeness gets in the way of real transcendence. Nonetheless, it does not belie the underlying desire to fill the emptiness that occurs and reoccurs and perhaps can only be satisfied when united in the infinite and eternal "Wholeness" that has its fulfillment in God.

In a sense, science seems to be affirming what human consciousness, across cultures, has always intuited. Physical evidence is pointing to something more, something sacred, something holy undergirding all of creation.

In his book *The Hidden Heart of the Cosmos*, the cosmologist Brian Swimme uses the phrase "all-nourishing abyss," to describe what can't be seen or even imagined in this quantum reality. He states it is "impossible to find any place in the universe that is outside this activity. Even in the darkest region beyond the Great Wall of Galaxies . . . even in the gaps between the synapses of the neurons in the brain, there occurs an incessant foaming, a flashing flame, a shining forth from and a dissolving back into.

Mystical experience, cosmic consciousness, and deep insight into truths not available to the intellect are areas of quantum investigation. Science and religion are in dialogue. The physics of the last fifty years has opened a window into a quantum realm that is allowing the wall between matter and spirit to be deconstructed. In its place is the vibrating field of resonating particles and waves that are evidence of the underlying oneness of the universe and everything in it, including consciousness.

The scientific revolution has challenged and refuted the death of God. Many tenets once held sacred have been revisited and revised, leading the scientific researcher Mc Taggert to write, "Far from destroying God, science for the first time was proving His existence—by demonstrating that a higher, collective consciousness was out there. There no longer need be two truths, the truth of science and the truth of religion. There could be one unified vision of the world."

Here, in a place that is not a place, time ceases to exist and each of us can access a dimension of consciousness deeper than thought, known in ancient teachings as the Christ within or one's Buddha nature.

The scientist Peter Russell, in his book *From Science to God: A Physicists Journey into the Mystery of Consciousness*, reminds us, "When we consider the writing of great saints and sages . . . when they talk of God . . . they are usually referring to a profound personal experience. . . . When we want to find God, we have to look within, into deep mind, a realm that Western science has yet to explore."

Does it matter what we call this God—Holy Spirit, Divine Light, the Beloved, Yahweh, Elohim, Brahman, Buddha nature, the Being behind All Creation, the More, the Sacred, Holy Mystery, Unified Field, Quantum Sea of Potential, All-Nourishing Abyss? We know that we know that we know. And that may be enough.

Theologian Karl Rahner questions if it may be necessary to get away from the very word G-O-D because it conjures up too limiting an image. This reverberates with the words of German theologian Meister Eckert, who said, "I pray to God to rid me of God," voicing the need to be freed from the images of God that are limited and constrained as they attempt to concretize or make tangible that which is unknowable.

Rahner writes in *The Practice of Faith*, "The concepts and words which we use are merely the tiny signs and idols which we erect so that they constantly remind us of the mystery . . . in which we reside." He suggests that God is not just a special piece of reality we can add to our naming and classifying systems. Rather, "that which we call God dwells in an unnamed and unsignposted expanse of our consciousness and is the comprehensive though never comprehended ground and presupposition of our experience and of the objects of that experience."

In my own journey, science has led me to theologians like Rahner, who have integrated the twenty- and twenty-first-century quantum discoveries into theology. Their work has released me from the exclusivity of images allocated to a particular faith community. They have liberated me from the image of a bearded figure, dressed in a white robe, sitting in the sky on a throne in everlasting judgment.

Letting go of G-O-D has allowed me to embrace metaphors that allow for the contributions of science to my spiritual journey, to consider the implications of quantum discoveries that led astrophysicist James Jeans to write in *The Mysterious Universe*, "The universe begins to look more like a great thought than a great machine. . . . Mind no longer appears as an accidental intruder into the realm of matter; we are beginning to suspect that we ought rather to hail it as the creator and governor of the realm of matter—not of course our individual minds, but the mind in which the atoms out of which our individual minds have grown exist as thoughts. . . . We discover that the universe shows evidence of a designing or controlling power that has something in common with our own individual minds."

The theologian Paul F. Knitter, in his book *Without Buddha I Could Not Be a Christian*, pulls it all together for me. He captures in a few sentences a concept of God that bridges the gap between the discoveries of science and religious intuition.

Knitter writes, "God is the field—the dynamic energy field of Inter-Being—in which 'we live and move and have our being' (Acts 17:28). Or from the divine perspective, there is 'one God above all things, through all things, and in all things' (Eph. 4:6)."

He goes on to say that this presence 'above, through, and in' can be imagined as an energy field pervading and influencing all that ever was, is, or will be. This seems to echo the scientific view put forth by Danah Zohar, when she suggests a God embodied within the quantum vacuum and using the laws of physics to be involved in a creative dialogue with the world.

Letting go of G-O-D led me back to the gospels, where I found in the teachings of Jesus Christ the very light and spirit that encompasses the whole of creation and allows for the timelessness that once terrified me.

The poet Kathleen Norris writes, "What we glimpse of the divine is always exactly enough and never enough."

Each revelation supplied by science has allowed me to add one more brushstroke to the canvas of my belief. The scale of ambivalence shifts as moments of holy presence emerge from the shadows of the implicate order and from the all-nourishing abyss. In that brief instance, everything is light.

ONCE IN THE MIDDLE of my life, the echo of that wholeness found me as a traveler and tourist in Helsinki, Finland. Bumping through the noonday traffic, we arrived at yet another church. I considered staying on the bus, for how many churches can you visit without reaching a point of diminishing return? I looked out the window of the bus for the requisite glimpse of spires and stained glass, perhaps a bell tower. But, no, it was the domed roof, rising like a giant mushroom out of a mountain of stone, that got me off the bus.

The church had been carved out of the granite that formed the underbelly of that city. The tour guide explained how billions of years of geological formations had produced a pink striated granite peninsula, creating the Baltic shield, which runs under the European continent.

It has been said that rocks hold the memory of earth's history. By measuring striations and radioactive decay, geologists can reconstruct timeframes that reach back into the earth's formation 4.5 billion years ago. They have determined that the red, purple and gray shades emanating from the Helsinki granite attest to the five hundred million years it took for this formation to evolve.

Initially a disc-shaped mass of dust and gas left over from the formation of the sun, our lush green planet first emerged as a massive ball of scorching liquid. Volcanoes and collision with other celestial bodies grew the planet. Eventually the outer layer cooled to form a solid crust as water began accumulating in the atmosphere. The molten heat at the earth's core is the engine that drove the creation of new rock. As land eroded, it was deposited as layers in the seas. Here the heat consolidated it into stone and uplifted it into new lands, which continued to bump and grind during the dark night of the planet's formation. A mere two billion years ago, mountains formed. The earth's crust folded and the first continents collided, and collided again, for as long as it took to create the Himalayas, the Rocky Mountains, Miami Beach, and Main Street.

Yet according to our tour guide, the relative lack of volcanic activity disturbing the Baltic Shield over the last four million years made the granite from which Helsinki's rock church was chiseled the oldest known rock on earth. As a result, we of the late twentieth century were standing on—and inside—the oldest rock on the planet.

While others bartered for glossy postcards and photographs of this rugged church, I found myself climbing onto the outcropping of rocks that rose like a moat surrounding the copper-domed roof of the church. Grasses and weeds poked their stalks out of the dirt the sun had baked to dust. Stray dogs roamed, occasionally stopping to urinate into the weeds. Children tested their balance as they barreled down the slope to the street. Other tourists, breathless like me, climbed the outcropping.

I encountered no signs or warnings about helping oneself to rocks. Even if there were, I would have pleaded innocent. Some impulse joined my need to hold a piece of this ancient granite in my hand. Not only hold it, but own it. And so I stooped as low as the dogs and scraped until I unearthed an obelisk of pink granite that filled me with the awareness that the skin cells on my hands and the sweat from my body were mingling with particles of a rock that had been a part of the earth from the earliest moments of its existence.

As I touched the carved wall, moisture from my palms mingled with the dust of the granite. The retina of my eyes absorbed the pink striated veins embedded in the stone. Four billion years was now.

The underlying connectedness of the physical universe with my body intersected in the stone. Time dissolved—anchoring me to first things, anchoring me to creation, anchoring me to God.

Chapter 29

The Final Story
In the Plaza

I N June of 2016, when I asked a friend to read the final draft of this manuscript, I arranged to deliver it to her at her office on the campus of Caldwell College. Since my graduation from Caldwell College in 1979, I had continued a close affiliation with the school, through groups I belonged to and personal relationships established over the years. As a result, I was frequently on campus.

On this particular day I walked across the plaza that I had walked through hundreds of times before. I was deep in thought. I had just come from having my blood drawn for the sixth time in as many months. Doctors were trying to diagnose what remained a mystery in the myriad symptoms manifesting in my body and in my blood work. I was very worried and had been for several months.

Preoccupied with and obsessing over what the ultimate diagnosis might reveal, I walked with my head down and my eyes on the ground.

I had advanced about three quarters of the way across the plaza that circled the building where my friend was waiting in her office to receive the manuscript. The plaza itself was constructed with stones, each about ten inches square. Some of the stones had been donated in memory of deceased loved ones. These were carved with the name and dates of birth and death and were set intermittently among the uncarved stones.

I was about two feet past one of the memorial stones when my mind registered the words my downcast eyes read as I stepped over it.

For Anna Winheim
My Mother

I backed up to check on what I thought I read, nearly tripping a couple of students walking behind me. Yes, there it was. I had not invented it. From the fog of memory, I remembered donating a small amount of money in remembrance of my mother when the plaza was constructed in the years following her death. I had totally forgotten about it. Although I had walked through the plaza hundreds of times, I never felt the need to find its placement in the pattern of the stones.

Now, seeing her name emerge from the stone, followed by the words "my mother," literally stopped me in my tracks. In that moment, the spell of my worry broke, and I was happy. Although I was tempted, there was no need to interpret it. One way or the other, I felt a nudge, to rest assured.

Questions for Discussion

Which story was most convincing to you in support of the author's thesis concerning the afterlife?

Do any stories seem farfetched? Does this weaken the concept?

Have you or a friend or relative ever had a similar experience to those recorded in the book?

Can the tension between science and religion ever be resolved?

Do we need a new vocabulary with which to speak about God, life after death, and the dying experience? Which scholars seem to find the right words?

Does science discredit religion in any way? Reinforce it?

Can there be a new "science of religion"? What would it mean for you?

Has reading this book changed any of your ideas about the life principle and what life after death may mean?

Bibliography

Abbot, Edwin. *Flatlands* (Wikipedia).

Alexandar, Eban, M.D. 2012. *Proof of Heaven: A Neurosurgeon's Journey into the Afterlife*. New York: Simon & Schuster.

Bohm, David. 1980. *Wholeness and the Implicate Order*. New York, Routledge & Keegan Paul.

Campbell, Joseph with Bill Moyers. 1988. *The Power of Myth*. New York, Doubleday.

Capra, Fritjof. 1999. *The Tao of Physics: 25th Anniversary Edition*. Boston: Shambala Publications.

Delio, Ilia. 2013. *The Unbearable Wholeness of Being*. New York: Orbis Books.

—— 2015. *Making All Things New: Catholicity, Cosmology, Consciousness*. New York: Orbis Books.

Dossey, Larry *Why Consciousness Is Not the Brain: The Science of Premonitions*. http://www.superconsciousness.com/topics/science/why-consciousness-not-brain.

Fiand, Barbara. 2008. *Awe Filled Wonder: The Interface of Science and Spirituality*. New York: Paulist Press.

—— 2006. *From Religion Back to Faith*. New York: Crossroads.

—— 2002. *In the Stillness You Will Know*. New York: Crossroad.

James, William. 2002. *The Varieties of Religious Experience*. London, Routladge.

Johnson, Elizabeth A. 2015. *Abounding in Kindness: Writings for the People of God*. New York: Orbis Books.

—— 2014. *Ask the Beasts: Darwin and the God of Love*. London: Bloomsbury Publishing.

—— 2008. "On This Holy Mountain." Leadership Council of Women Religious and CMSM Assembly. Denver.

Kelly, Edward F., Kelly, Emily Williams, Crabtree III, Adam, et al. 2007. *Irreducible Mind: Toward a Psychology for the 21st Century*. Maryland: Lanham: Rowman & Littlefield Publishers, Inc.

Knitter, Paul F. 2009. *Without Buddha I Could Not Be a Christian*. London: Oneworld Publications.

Koestler, Arthur. 1972. *The Roots of Coincidence*. New York: Random House.

Mc Enerny, Bonnie. *Messages Signs, Visits, and Premonitions from Loved Ones Lost on 9/11*. 2010. New York: William Morrow.

Mc Taggart, Lynne. 2008. *The Field: The Quest for the Secret Force of the Universe*. New York: Harper Collins.

O'Murchu, Diarmuid. 2012. *In the Beginning Was the Spirit*. New York: Orbis Books.

Russell, Peter. 2002. *Science to God: A Physicist's Journey into the Mystery of Consciousness*. Novato, California. New World Library.

Sheldrake, Rupert. 2013. *"The Sun."* Chapel Hill. North Carolina.

Stearn, Jess. 1973. *Search for a Soul*. New York: Doubleday & Company, Inc.

Swimme, Brian. 1996. *The Hidden Heart of the Cosmos*. New York: Orbis Books.

Teilhard de Chardin, Pierre. 1969. *How I Believe*. London: William Collins Sons & Co.,Ltd.

—— *Teilhard for Beginners: The Divine Milieu Explained*. http://www.teilhardforbeginners.com.

Tyson, Neil De Grasse. *Hemispheresmagazine.com*. March 2015.

Wessels, Cletus. 2003. *Jesus in the New Universe Story*. New York: Orbis Books.

Wiman, Christian. 2013. *My Bright Abyss: Meditations of a Modern Belief*. New York: Farraar, Straus and Giroux.

Yates, Jenny Ed. 1999. *Jung on Death and Immortality*. New Jersey: Princeton University Press.

Zohar, Danah. 1990. *The Quantum Self: Human Nature and Consciousness Defined by the New Physics*. New York: Quill/William Morrow.